Praise for

"Stuart [Higginbotham is ~~~~~
wrong and young enough to believe things can change when people
stop trying to lead the Spirit and start yielding instead. How does
such a high vision become a trustworthy reality on the ground?
Read this book to find out."

—**Barbara Brown Taylor**, author, *An Altar in the World*
and *Holy Envy: Finding God in the Faith of Others*

"Can our parishes become places where the heart's desire for God can
be aroused and God's desire for us actually experienced in our common life? Can mindfulness and practices grounded in the wisdom
of the contemplative tradition transform the ethos of our troubled
communities? Those who hope that the answer is a Spirit-inspired
YES will find encouragement in this deeply encouraging and accessi-
ble account of a vision put into realistic contemporary practice."

—**The Rev. Martin Smith**, renowned spiritual
director; author, *The Word Is Very Near You*

"With courage and creativity, Stuart Higginbotham applies a transformed vision to an unlikely arena of contemplative engagement:
parish administration. . . . He invites [us] to relinquish facile, anxiety-driven quick fixes . . . or the compulsion to 'get the job done.'
Instead, [he] shows how a contemplative approach can illuminate
and free every aspect of parish life."

—**The Rev. Julia Gatta, PhD**, Bishop Frank A. Juhan Professor of Pastoral
Theology, the School of Theology, the University of the South, Sewanee

"As much a practical guide as a treasure trove of wisdom. . . .
Explores not only what it means to be a Christian contemplative
in the world but [also] how mindfulness practice can radically
transform what we think of as parish leadership, discernment, and
ministry. . . . As timely as it is urgent."

—**Fr. Vincent Pizzuto, PhD**, University of San Francisco; author,
Contemplating Christ: The Gospels and the Interior Life

"Do you long for the fresh winds of the Spirit to blow through your church? Read this book. It refreshed and inspired me, and left me full of imaginative possibilities."

—**Margaret Benefiel, PhD**, author, *Crisis Leadership* and *The Soul of Leadership*; executive director, the Shalem Institute for Spiritual Formation

"Invites and challenges congregational life to listen, trust, and move ever more deeply into the life that God desires for the Christian community and the world."

—**Jessica Smith, PhD**, co-editor, *Contemplation and Community: A Gathering of Fresh Gathering for a Living Tradition*

"Provides a map for congregational questions, discernment, and action amid change. Through innovative exercises, a range of prayer practices, and study, clergy, parishioners, and seekers learn to open to Spirit-born/Spirit-led insight and innovation."

—**The Rev. Bobbi Patterson, PhD**, Episcopal priest; professor emerita, Emory University Religion Department; author, *Building Resilience Through Contemplative Practice*

"Contemplative reformation in action. . . . Inspiring his vestry and church community to ponder their vocation as clergy and laity, Higginbotham observes how a new spaciousness invites a radical awareness of God's love and calling."

—**Lerita Coleman Brown, PhD,** spiritual director; author, *When the Heart Speaks, Listen*

"Stuart Higginbotham knows both the joys and challenges of a truly contemplative ministry, and the wisdom he shares in this book will help clergy and congregational leaders to thrive as they share their contemplative heart with others."

—**Carl McColman**, author, *Eternal Heart* and *The Big Book of Christian Mysticism*

"In an age when spirituality centers and mystical path coaches abound for individuals and groups, could a whole congregation take a more contemplative path? This is the story of how Stuart Higginbotham and Grace Episcopal Church . . . are discovering that the contemplative wisdom of our Christian tradition honors the work of the Spirit in bringing about a new and more sustainable life for the future."

—**Fr. Guerric Heckel, OCSO**, St. Francis Retreat Center Director, Mepkin Abbey, Moncks Corner, SC

"A wellspring of wisdom. Herein lies crucial insight and instruction for the evolving church. Every despairing clergy will be nourished and inspired by this important contribution for congregational life."

—**Phileena Heuertz**, founding partner, Gravity, a Center for Contemplative Activism; author, *Mindful Silence* and *Pilgrimage of a Soul*

"A vital and badly needed contribution to both clergy and laypeople who care about what it means to go deeper together as a church, responding to the invitations of God's Spirit in Christ."

—**The Rev. Tilden Edwards, PhD**, founder and senior fellow, the Shalem Institute for Spiritual Formation; author, *Embracing the Call to Spiritual Depth: Gifts for Contemplative Living*

The Heart of a Calling

The Practice of Christian Mindfulness in Congregational Ministry

STUART HIGGINBOTHAM

A Crossroad Book
The Crossroad Publishing Company

New York

The Crossroad Publishing Company www.crossroadpublishing.com

© 2021 by Stuart Higginbotham

Crossroad, Herder & Herder, and the crossed C logo/colophon are registered trademarks of The Crossroad Publishing Company.

Book design by Tim Holtz

Library of Congress Cataloging-in-Publication Data available from the Library of Congress.

ISBN (trade paperback) 9780824597030
ISBN (epub) 9780824597078

Books published by The Crossroad Publishing Company may be purchased at special quantity discount rates for classes and institutional use. For information, please email sales@crossroadpublishing.com.

With enormous thanks for the people of Grace Episcopal Church.

Contents

Introduction

This book is about vocation, what it means to be called to a life of prayer and service both as a clergy person and as a community. As we reflect on this together, let me begin by being vulnerable with you and sharing a dream I had in August 2018.

Some two months before Fr. Thomas Keating died, I went to sleep one night and had a powerful dream that continues to help nurture my sense of vocation as a parish priest. I only met Fr. Thomas once, over the course of five days, as part of the New Contemplative Exchange gathering at St. Benedict's Monastery in Snowmass, Colorado, in August 2017. Twenty young contemplative scholars, clergy, and practitioners were invited to share together in a series of conversations alongside Fr. Thomas, Richard Rohr, Laurence Freeman, and Tilden Edwards. Our shared hope was to listen for what the Spirit was saying about next steps in the broader Christian contemplative fellowship that we all shared.

In my dream, I had been invited to visit Fr. Thomas. I was with a small group, but I didn't know who any of the others were. I couldn't see the faces of the people in the group, but I felt them there. We were at what I felt was a monastery, and there was a small cabin there, a lovely little building, surrounded by gardens and grass. Strangely, I was carrying a tuba.

When we walked up to the cabin, another monk was there at the door. He was not Trappist, but he had on a simple white alb or cassock. He had white hair but seemed young. He opened the door, welcomed us all in, and showed us to a small waiting room on the side of the cabin. One by one we were going to see Fr. Thomas.

The monk called for me, and as we walked into the room with Fr. Thomas, he was lying there in his Trappist habit on a sort of daybed in the middle of the room. The monk said, "Fr. Thomas, here is Stuart."

"Oh yes, Stuart," he said. "Please come over here. We need to talk."

I walked over and sat next to him, on the edge of the bed. He leaned up a bit and said, "Are you ready to receive your marching orders for what comes next? For what you are supposed to do?" I told him I was. I felt unsure of what was going to come next.

Suddenly there were other people in the room. They felt like observers, but I didn't really see them. They were in the background, watching.

Fr. Thomas raised up his hands and said, "By the power vested in me from the governor of Georgia and to the republic for which it stands." I thought that was very odd.

Then Fr. Thomas looked at me, leaned in close, winked and smiled, and said, "We need to do this showy stuff. They like this, don't they?" We both smiled at each other and then it was just the two of us. Everyone else had suddenly faded away.

He leaned toward me with a serious look on his face. He said, "Now, are you really ready to know what you are supposed to do? Who you are?"

"I think so," I told him. "Yes."

Fr. Thomas became very focused. He reached up, made the sign of the cross on each of my eyes, and looked intently in my face.

"You are to remain as simple as possible, to be a teacher, and to show all whom you meet that God is already with them and loves them." After he said this, we both just sat there with each other. We looked at each other, and he asked me, "Do you understand what I am telling you?"

"Yes," I told him, "I understand."

"Good" he said.

He smiled, lay back down, and I shot straight up in bed awake. It was 1:55 a.m. when I looked at my phone.

This dream continues to influence how I understand my vocation as a parish priest in the world we live in. "Do you understand what I am telling you?" Fr. Thomas said. I am still trying to do so, and I believe I will yearn for a fuller understanding my entire life.

I am a simple parish priest who struggles to make sense of a life of prayer within the demands of an institution. For a good long while, the traditional institutional church has experienced decline, and this reality has sparked countless anxious conversations—and plans to fix the problem. Some cannot imagine "church" looking any other way than how they have experienced it in the last few decades. To even broach the conversation feels like a betrayal of the legacy many have inherited. There is much anxiety and fear, yet there is also enormous opportunity to practice a deeper degree of trust in the movement of the living Spirit. How am I called to be a priest today?

I am blessed to be a priest in the midst of enormous shifts in the way we understand ourselves as interconnected human beings in community, even as these tensions cause enormous stress. While many people have become so frustrated with the institutional or traditional parish church, I count myself blessed to serve in a community that is dedicated to being transformed into the likeness of Christ. Are there frustrations and resistances? Of course. As my parish looks toward its bicentennial celebration, there is understandably pride in what the community has experienced. Some feel quite bound to the structures and customs we have known. Humanity will be what humanity will be; however, my years as a parish priest have also shown me glimpses that humanity can be what God desires it to be.

As I write this introduction, we have been home for over eight months in a time of global pandemic, with the pressures of an economic downturn, a toxic election season, and the complex potential for seeking healing in our history of racial injustice. "Church" has taken on a whole new meaning for many, and many are frustrated that they are not able to worship the way they always have worshipped. We have been removed from our predictable patterns, and this absence may just be the gracious gift we have been waiting for to enable our souls to stretch into new ways of imagining what it means to be the Body of Christ today. How to be a priest in times such as these?

For twelve years I have been blessed by conversation partners who have helped me delve more deeply into my sense of call, my practice of ministry. I dare say that every minister has their own collection of colleagues and practices that are drawn from the centuries of wisdom we have all inherited. The specific experiences and insights I will share in this book all center on the vocational discernment I continue to experience. For almost twenty years I have explored how the wisdom of the Christian contemplative tradition connects with the contemporary interest in mindfulness in the broader culture. My own initial experience with mindfulness practice nurtured a deepening sense of what an integrated mind-in-heart practice of prayer could be in my life and the life of my Christian community. What is driving this interest in mindfulness practice today? What pressures in the broader culture are sparking a deeper desire for practices of paying attention in the midst of busyness, competition, and consumption? What might the Christian contemplative tradition have to say to these deeper questions?

How I understand my own vocation as a priest in the church lies at the heart of this particular work. Each chapter reflects on key themes that have caught my eye and nurtured my heart as I consider how the church is called to delve more deeply into practices of prayer and spiritual imagination in this time of challenge and invitation. I will explore key images within the context of the gathered congregation, praying that the Spirit can open us to a deeper awareness of what is possible for a renewal of our common vocation. We have an enormous heritage of prayer and practice whose depths can speak to the challenges we face today, yet we so often persist in merely skating across the surface. How can we take the risks to engage more deeply in our common prayer so that our lives are renewed with a deeper trust in the Spirit's movement among us and within us? How might such a deeper exploration of the Christian contemplative tradition reorient the way we embody ministry in the parish church in the midst of the challenges we face today?

This book is grounded in vulnerable self-reflection and prayer. My hope is not to stay in my head but rather to speak from my heart. At the end of the day, telling the story of my life in community is the only way I know how to describe what I am still trying to make sense of myself. Many others have written much more eloquent and scholarly treatises on the intricate interaction between Christian and Buddhist beliefs and practices. Many others are experts in the latest developments of church administration and leadership frameworks. I am enormously grateful to many whose work has enriched my own evolving ministry. I am very aware that what I am offering is contingent and limited, yet I can still tell this story of how I have experienced God's grace and the potential for what I see as a contemplative reformation in the traditional parish church. Perhaps you will find it meaningful. I offer no plans or products that "work"; rather, I only offer my story and my struggles in seeking and searching for a way to live into my vocation in such challenging days.

Each of us has a vocation, a particular way that God is calling us to share our gifts in the world. Throughout both his letters to the church in Corinth, St. Paul reminded the community there of this reality, and his words ring in our ears as well. We are all called to cultivate an awareness of how God is calling us to participate in the mystery that is life and ministry today, in these extremely challenging times. We are in the midst of an enormous reorientation in the way we understand church and ministry. We can draw on the wisdom of our tradition and sages throughout the centuries as we continue our own path of discernment and embodiment in the world today.

With Gratitude

Becoming aware of one's vocation—and living into it—is a lifelong journey with many twists and turns. I have been blessed with soul friends who continue to encourage me to pay attention to the presence of God in my life. In particular, I want to thank Tilden Edwards, Barbara Brown Taylor, Julia Gatta, Martin Smith, Vincent Pizzuto, Jessie Smith, Margaret Benefiel, Bobbi Patterson, Lerita Coleman Brown, Guerric Heckel, Carl McColman, Courtney Cowart, Jim Goodmann, Adam Bucko, Justin Lanier, Rebecca Parker, Maggie Winfrey, Sarah Bachelard, and Phileena Heuertz. I will be forever grateful for you.

I am blessed to be able to work each day with an incredible team at Grace Episcopal Church, and the entire community in Northeast Georgia is filled with extraordinary and compassionate souls. The staff, vestry, and congregation at Grace inspires me each day to be a better priest and person. In particular, thank you to Cynthia Park, Kathy Gosselin, Becky Whitmire, Cheryl Kelley, and Jason Voyles for your willingness to share your stories. Thank you all, from the bottom of my heart.

I am also enormously grateful for Gwendolin Herder, Emily Wichland, Nadia Santos, and the entire team at Crossroad Publishing. Their willingness to explore this book in the midst of the pandemic helped give me the courage to take next steps.

As always, of course, I am so thankful for Lisa and Evelyn, my harbor and my heart, with whom I am honored to share a life.

1
Context and the Challenge

*Spiritual freedom occurs when we become
aware of our limits through leaving them behind.
Mystical ecstasy means to discover the limiting
of the spirit and to cross over the imposed limits.
Only in seeing again do I know that I was blind;
that I was squatting in a prison becomes apparent
only when the prison door opens.*

—**Dorothee Soelle**, *The Silent Cry*

When I arrived at Grace Episcopal Church seven years ago, I saw the
same basic leadership structure as exists in most church communities:
rector, parish administrative staff, program staff, and a vestry whose
members were organized as de facto department heads of the various
ministries and committees. I was looking to hire an associate priest in
the next nine or ten months, and I knew that decision would give me
an opportunity to further develop the range of our clerical responsi-
bilities and ministries.

Ours was a rigid structure in many ways, but the very rigidity lent
itself to a comfortable predictability. New vestry members were seated
each January, replacing those who rotated off, to work with committees to maintain the various ministries and opportunities the community supported. The staff continued to make sure that the finances,

communication, and building management aspects were taken care of. I quickly realized that my role could easily focus solely on maintaining this organizational structure, working with my parish administrator and senior warden to make sure all the ministries were supported— while the parish members were made adequately aware of the entire enterprise so to continue with their pledges.

I would vouch that my situation mirrored many if not most others in the church. I experienced a well-known model that I had come to describe in previous parish experiences as the "program-maintenance model" of congregational and spiritual leadership. So long as the programs were effectively maintained and ample communication and pastoral care were provided, the parish's ministries could indeed continue. But was there a more dynamic, Spirit-conscious way of sharing in spiritual and congregational leadership? Was there a way to embody a degree of risky faithfulness within our common life that invited the entire community into a space of shared ministry and vocational discernment?

When I was in the search process, I was very open about my interest in contemplative leadership and practices. I told the committee about my time with the Shalem Institute for Spiritual Formation and how grateful I was for Tilden Edwards's challenge to trust explicitly in the Holy Spirit's guidance and presence within a church community—and within all of life. Edwards and I had shared many conversations about what it might be like to become even more conscious of the Spirit's presence within the life of a community of prayer. I opened up and told both the search committee and the vestry about my hopes for a "way of being a rector" that was more intentional in practices of prayer, in community-centered discernment, and in a way of being together that fostered appreciation and participation within the entire parish. I spoke of how I saw the profound tradition of Benedictine spirituality as an inspiring guide for our own development as a church—a church that wanted to move, in organizational language, from being a program-sized church to a resource-sized congregation centered in prayer and worship.

The committees were sincerely interested. They were excited about exploring new possibilities, and they were curious about what such a spacious and Spirit-conscious approach might be like in the particular context of Grace Church. As excited as I was by their curiosity and interest, I also cautioned them that such a communal endeavor would carry enormous risk. It would ask for a level of vulnerability and communication that, heretofore, may have been lacking. It would entail developing new skills and a willingness to become more proficient in our own theological language and ability to articulate our encounters with God's presence. It would require us to identify places of resistance even as we reminded ourselves of our belief that the Holy Spirit was inviting us to respond even more fully into what the baptismal rite in the 1979 *Book of Common Prayer* describes as our call to "grow into the full stature of Christ" (BCP, 302).

I remained curious about the Grace community and our common interest throughout our conversations over the eight months of the search process. During that time, we grew closer to one another in this deep, trusting communication. They spoke with me about their frustration at feeling stagnant, and I shared my hope to lean into a practice of spiritual leadership that was indeed beckoning me. I expressed my hope and prayer to hold such risk and vulnerability as they conveyed their intention to support an imaginative space of shared leadership and spiritual reflection. When they invited me to be their rector, I felt empowered to step into this space we had imagined together. When I went to see the bishop the next morning, his first response to me was, "This is going to be extremely interesting."

Personal Testimonies

To gain a wider perspective on the experience of the search process, I invited three former senior wardens, each of whom was serving on the vestry that called me, to share their thoughts on how they hoped, dreamed, and wrestled in the search process and the transition time. When I was called to be the rector of Grace Church, I was the twenty-seventh in a long line of missioners, vicars, priests-in-charge, and rectors over a history of almost two centuries. Each of these remarkable individuals helped me see the opportunity for shared leadership grounded in prayer and discernment. Their reflections on the search process show how the vestry was hopeful and aware of the parish's potential.

First is a reflection from the Hon. Kathy Gosselin, the senior warden who invited me to come to Grace. Kathy's presence meant so much to me when I first arrived. Due to the timing of Grace's annual meeting, Kathy rotated off the vestry one month after I arrived, yet we continued to meet. Her support and counsel were vital during that first year of my cure—and continue to be so.

When I was senior warden during the search process, much of the initial work was prescribed for us by the diocese. So my job involved administrative work to make sure we scheduled the meetings with candidates in a timely fashion and at such time that all members of the vestry could be present. All vestry members completed their homework of reviewing all the material about each candidate. Then I ensured we had our questions prepared, and we decided which vestry member would ask them for each candidate's visit. This work was extensive and detailed, and it was entered into thoughtfully, mindfully, and with prayer. I asked Cheryl, one of our members, to start our sessions as a vestry and our interviews with the candidates with prayer, to focus us appropriately. But this preparatory work, for me, was not something out of the ordinary.

Once we had concluded the visits with all three candidates, my challenges began. I believe I spent more concentrated time in conversation with the Spirit during this phase than at any other time in my life. I also shared my thoughts and vision with other members of the

*vestry, who aided and guided me with great suggestions. The evening
we were to meet to decide on our new rector needed to be one of serious, careful, open, and calm discussion leading to consensus. Shaping
the evening so as to make sure we were guided by God as well as one
another was a daunting task. And knowing we were doing this for the
entire parish made it all that much more of a consuming conversation
in my head. We were presented with very diverse candidates, appeal-
ing to different members of the vestry, and I wanted to make sure
everyone was heard and all aspects of the decision were considered.
As the weeks passed by, I wanted to make sure we could all recall
the details of our first meeting. I made posters of the notes I'd taken
after the interviews, with feedback from all vestry members. These
included each candidate's strengths and challenges. I also decided that
we would pass around a ball of yarn that each person speaking would
hold while they spoke. This meant they could not be interrupted.
(Yarn is important to me, and we were meeting in my knitting
room.) I tried to prepare for any questions I could put to the group
to have them look deeply at this decision, without trying to focus on
a particular candidate. And I kept alert throughout the evening's
conversation in order to catch the Spirit in action, pointing it out as
subtly as I could. (Wow, that sounds way more intentional than it
was.) I felt a heavy weight of responsibility to be "on," guiding us to a
decision that brought joy and peace to our expectations. Cheryl started
our evening with wonderful prayer and reading, and each member
spoke politely about their views. After four hours we were agreed in
our decision. I feel this may have been one of the times I actually experienced the peace of the Lord and was aware of it. The evening had a
very organic feel to it, if that makes sense. It was a great privilege to
serve in this way. Calling the bishop, calling Stuart, and announcing
the decision at church were just the delights I was fortunate to savor
after our critical evening. My delight was well founded as every year
since Stuart started at Grace has been a blessing.*

Next is a reflection from Becky Whitmire, my second senior warden
and former coordinator of pastoral care at the parish. Becky's presence
continues to ground me and those who work with her. Her calming
spirit was reassuring during the year she served as senior warden.

*As I think back on the search process that brought Stuart to Grace
Church, the first thing that comes to mind is my initial concern over
who we as a vestry would choose to serve on the search committee.
While it was important to choose a diverse group of parishioners in
terms of their ministry involvement and experience at Grace, I also
felt it extremely important that those chosen be good listeners and
able to work well together. As it turned out, I was quite happy about
those who were chosen for the committee and felt confident that they
would do a good job of choosing candidates.*

*Once the search committee handed the selection process over to the
vestry, my concern moved to my own personal ability to be true to
the needs of the congregation as expressed through the parish survey
as well as to those needs of which I was aware through my vestry
involvement. In addition to the attributes every church is looking
for (someone who can inspire, teach, grow the church, etc.), it was
important that Grace find a rector with strong personal engagement, pastoral care, conflict resolution, and personnel management
abilities. The good news is that the search committee provided three
very strong candidates. The vestry agreed that either of two of those
candidates would be a good fit, although in different ways. Stuart
was at the beginning of his career, and the concern was about both
his depth of experience and the response he might receive from the
(many) older Grace parishioners who might discount him because of
his age. The other candidate had many years in the priesthood and
would be well received by the congregation in terms of his personality
and experience, but the concern for me was that if he was not able to
inject energy where needed, then we would continue on as an older,*

shrinking congregation. In making our final decision, there was much talk about the difference in age and experience of the candidates. What it kept coming back to for me, though, was the excitement I felt about Stuart and his answers to our questions during his formal interview with the vestry. I remember thinking that that excitement would most probably translate to very good things for Grace Church, and so it has.

Last is a reflection from Cheryl Kelley, my third senior warden. After rotating off the vestry, Cheryl and I continued having conversations about opportunities for spiritual formation and Christian education at Grace. When a staff position opened up, I was able to invite her to be Grace's new director of Christian formation.

My three-year term on the vestry began just as the search committee finished the parish profile and began receiving applications. I felt honored to be asked to serve at such an important transitional time, and I took that responsibility seriously. It was weighty and exciting at the same time!

Our search committee did an excellent job recruiting and screening candidates, and ultimately recommended three candidates for the vestry's consideration. They refused to endorse any one of them over the others—insisting that any one of the candidates would be a good choice. And they were right. Each candidate brought different gifts: one had obvious administrative strengths; one had a huge pastoral presence; and one had a kind of joyful enthusiasm that was infectious. The last one was obviously Stuart.

I was looking for someone who could breathe new life into the parish. We had been in a holding pattern for a long time, and we needed someone who could attract new people and reengage existing ones. It was obvious to me that Stuart had the kind of personality that was perfect for that, and I really liked some of the creative things he had done at his previous parish. I read his earlier notes on what he called the Obedire Project, and I was very intrigued. I thought it sounded much like what I had been hearing parishioners say they were hungry for. He had enjoyed great success growing his previous parish and engaging new, young families. I thought he had what Grace needed.

The part that made it feel risky was that he was so young and had never served as rector before—ever! Not just never at a parish our size. There was concern about whether he could manage the staff and difficult personnel issues. There was concern about whether he would have the necessary credibility with the older members of our parish. There was concern about maintaining our "traditional" sense of liturgy and worship. Stuart gave us examples of some his experiences that spoke to those issues, but he'd never really done what we would be asking him to do. We were all intrigued by the possibility we saw in Stuart, but it was equal parts exciting and scary.

I felt the Holy Spirit nudging us along in the whole process, creating a sense of calm under everybody's "what ifs." The tipping point came, though, when near the end of our final voting meeting, our senior warden asked, "When you imagine calling a candidate, which one makes you feel excited about Grace's future?" The answer was unanimously Stuart. A sense of recognition, then calm, filled the room. We had our answer.

Listening Circles

When I arrived at Grace on the Feast of the Epiphany in 2014, my calendar was filled with folks who wanted to visit. They wanted to share their stories of pain and disappointment in twenty years of complex and sometimes troubled leadership as well as their hopes for a new time of refreshment, growth, imagination, and joy. Over dozens of pots of tea, we entered into a period of listening together. I was vividly aware of how my role as their rector could "set a tone," as I had heard it described. Rather than rushing in to identify problems and suggest changes, I invited them to dream with me.

From my time with Shalem—and in my own spiritual practice and conversations with both Christians and Buddhists over the years—I had become interested in mindfulness practice. I began reflecting with parishioners on how mindfulness practice might, indeed, be a way to enter into a shared conversation around ministry and congregational life. We approached mindfulness in the terms of renowned teacher Bhante Gunaratana. That is, we asked ourselves how we might share a certain degree of "non-egoistic alertness" and an "awareness of change"[1] when it came to our shared ministry in the parish. I invited them to risk reflecting on our common life in a way that connected intriguingly with Gunaratana's definition of mindfulness:

> It is observing the passing flow of experience. It is watching things as they are changing. It is seeing the birth, growth, and maturity of all phenomena. It is watching the phenomena decay and die. Mindfulness is watching things, moment by moment, continuously.[2]

When it came to their past experiences as a parish community, how were they aware of areas of growth, struggle, invitation, resistance? How were they aware of their desires, fears, and hopes? How could we practice together and learn to share these insights with one another as a parish? As Gunaratana suggests, "Mindfulness is participatory observation. The meditator is both participant and observer at one and the same time."[3]

Beginning the first month, I invited the entire parish into a four-months-long series of weekly conversations. These "listening circles" were designed to foster relationships as much as to find clarity and direction. Each Wednesday, for ten weeks, over a hundred people gathered around tables in the parish hall to share dinner together. Each week, I invited them to consider a question: "As a member of the community of Grace Episcopal Church, what have been your most meaningful experiences with ____?" Together we explored the many areas of our common life, from pastoral care to choir and music to community ministry partnerships to children's ministries.

They sat in small groups, and one person in each group recorded what was shared so that we could find a way to gather the many images of ministry—wondering how the Spirit's guidance would be perceived. I encouraged them to speak honestly and deeply while avoiding any urge to vent about what simply frustrated them. I told them that we would not carry forward any comments that were rooted in anger or frustration but only those that could foster dialogue and our call to live into our baptismal covenant as a community of faith. Knowing their history as a community pitted against itself after affairs and mistrust, I acknowledged that I knew they could sabotage this process at any time. I also admitted that I could sabotage this as well by yielding to any impulse within myself to revert to a more business-centered leadership style whereby I simply made decisions rather than listening deeply to how the Spirit of Christ was at work within our shared community. We were being invited to trust and risk.

Over these weeks we listened, we spoke, we shared meals, and we grew to trust more deeply. We heard stories of pain and loss illumined by hope and love. We learned that we could step into a space of vulnerability and honesty. We paid attention—we were mindful—of how we felt. We were curious, and we realized what a gift that truly was.

At the end of the ten weeks, we had collected almost two hundred pages of handwritten notes, dreams, stories, and ideas, and we compiled all these into a binder to use for further discernment and reflection. We wondered together, "How do we see the Spirit of Christ leading us and inviting us?" Immediately, a few areas came into focus: greater community partnerships in the city and wider area, deeper pastoral awareness, the need for further work to foster trust within the parish community, and the opportunity to develop a rich space of creative expression within our shared ministries.

We quickly learned that such mindfulness practice—as embodied within this shared experience—enabled us to focus both on what the community had experienced in the past as well as how we were being invited to step into the future. We had become more aware of those things that had wounded the community, those experiences that had impeded spiritual growth, and the attitudes and behaviors that we needed to release. In other words, mindfulness practice was a practice through which parishioners might engage in the dynamic of conversion within the community's life.

Remarkably, if there was one focus point that repeatedly arose during the conversations, it was the opportunity for creative expression, for the cultivation of imagination in all areas of the parish's common life. Grace is a community that contains many artists: painters, sculptors, writers, poets, dramatists, musicians, and singers. It is a place full of wonder and experimentation, and all of those gathered in the small group conversations immediately noticed how this was a dominant theme woven into many of the community's various ministries and committees. Recognizing this common point, we intentionally held it up as a charism of our community. It is an element of faith that inspires every aspect of our shared life, and we pledged ourselves to find ways to participate imaginatively with this dimension of the Spirit's call on our life.

The entire community realized we had the opportunity to anchor our ministry within such an imaginative endeavor. They did not want this to be some tangential activity or merely some vague, ethereal element within the details of ministry and life. Rather, they desired to seek ways to live imaginatively, to pray imaginatively, to worship imaginatively, and to manage imaginatively. The staff and vestry realized that, if we were to embody the discernment of the community more fully, we were being called to reimagine how we organized the very leadership framework of the parish.

After praying about our shared discernment experience and wondering about ways to reorient our leadership framework, the next vestry election gave us the opportunity to embody it. We worked as a staff and vestry to plan a transition from the more traditional management structure to one that was centered in a mindful, imaginative, and creative space. Whereas the prior vestry and staff configurations were configured on the program-maintenance model, aligned with various ministry departments such as pastoral care, outreach, children and youth, and stewardship, we wondered what it might be like to structure our ministries into collaborative networks we called "ministry clusters." These clusters would foster the ongoing imaginative, collaborative, and discernment-based work that the small-group listening circles had begun.

After praying with the two hundred pages of notes about our conversations, we identified five broad areas of ministry within the Grace community: Administration, Compassion, Formation, Participation, and Liturgy & Creative Expression. We purposefully noted how worship and prayer—our Common Prayer—weave throughout all of the clusters and continually invite us into a greater awareness of God's love for us. Every ministry we have at Grace finds an anchor in one of these cluster spaces. The vestry and staff resonate with various ones of them as they work together to invite the entire parish to share their gifts and experience our common identity as part of the Body of Christ.

To help organize our life, I asked five key staff members to function as coordinators for the clusters, based on their ministry role and gifts. The vestry members reorganized themselves into the clusters (either one or two) based on their interest, gifts, and skills, rather than focusing solely on one aspect of the parish's life. For example, the Outreach vestry liaison became a crucial member of the Compassion Cluster and the Stewardship vestry chairperson serves on the Administration Cluster. Rather than only going to meetings that pertain solely to their specific committee, the clusters regularly meet together and share ideas on how the various ministries within them are connected. Immediately, the Outreach and Pastoral Care committees realized that they both were seeking to embody Christ's compassion in the world, albeit it in two different focus points. After meeting together, they realized they had never before understood how we are called to live into concentric circles of compassion within our parish, city, state, and global communities.

When the new vestry class arrived, one of their first decisions was to create a new "seat" on the vestry specifically for Creative Expression. They realized how meaningful it would be to have a vestry member present at every meeting to remind us to lean more into our imaginative vocation. The traditional Buildings and Grounds vestry position was eliminated and was replaced with a liaison for a reoriented Campus Vision and Development Committee. The former Stewardship chairperson realized that he actually resonated with the Participation Cluster and its hope to foster greater involvement from the entire community just as much as he did with the Administration Cluster and its focus on the financial health of the parish. Greater connections were made between the entire vestry and staff team, and we entered into a time of deep conversations. To help coordinate all this reorientation and support the conversations, the Senior Warden's role became a key focus point. This person worked (and continues to work) alongside me in fostering communication, coordinating planning, and enabling even greater participation from the entire community. Together, we make an incredible team!

To be sure, we utilized many flow charts and graphs that helped lay out the logistics of this transition. We made sure that everyone was comfortable with the details of the structure, and we continually clarified expectations with staff, vestry, and ministry chair persons throughout the community. Transitions are never easy, yet this one has truly fostered a stronger connection with parishioners.

Transition and Embodiment

The transition into such a leadership model has not been entirely easy.
We have shared many conversations around expectations and the risk
entailed when we move from a well-known framework to one that
feels much more vulnerable. Some in the parish wondered why any
reorientation was necessary, while others welcomed it wholeheartedly. When I invited the Rev. Dr. Cynthia Park to share this work
with me as my associate, I shared with her my hopes for continuing
this exploration of a mindful way of embodying leadership within the
community. She brought invaluable insights from her background as
both a therapist as well as a Biblical scholar with a doctorate from
the Catholic University of America. Her reflection on her experience
helping shape this mindful leadership model are insightful:

*I was deep into the interviewing process with two other congregations
on the day Stuart called. "Hey, friend. I need you." For months I
had danced something between the Seven Veils and the Tango with
these different search committees, each "side" trying to read between
the lines, frame things positively, and figure out whether "this" might
work. When I heard Stuart's voice, my soul resonated with the possibility of sharing a yoke with a wondrously grounded colleague. I
accepted the invitation to join him without ever hearing any details
about what he wanted me to do or be. I was in the process of moving from Atlanta to Gainesville before a colleague told me he'd seen
my job title in the diocesan news. "Apparently you are going to be in
charge of something called 'ministries of compassion.'"*

*Stuart's vision of "mindful church" unfolded for me after I arrived
during the course of heart-to-heart conversations about our lives and
our vocations. I answered his invitation to come join him not because
I was impressed by his ideas but because I was impressed by his life,
his character, and his generosity. Many older and more experienced*

*rectors are famously stingy and territorial about sharing parish
ministry. Capable of doing so many things well, Stuart is surprisingly
generous with ministry and praise—not just with his clergy colleagues
but with every leader in the congregation. I am convinced that it is
this generosity of spirit that allows room for others to imagine, and
imagination is, I believe, the essential resource needed for mindful
practice to be generative.*

*Even so, in practical terms, his "mindful church" model appeared
cumbersome to me, at the beginning. I had been trained to exercise
more authoritative and individual leadership by fiat, which appeared
to have the effect of greater efficiency. What I came to realize is that
this appearance of efficiency comes at the high cost of limited personal
investment from parishioners. Under Stuart's model, consensus building derives from a period of mutual discernment and prayer. Initially,
I experienced this as needlessly slow and inefficient. Within the first
quarter, however, my experience of personal investment on the part
of the parishioners percolated to the surface. This positive culture of
personal investment in an idea or a program accomplished three
necessary achievements that are historically hard to achieve under
the model with which I was more familiar. The first is that folks are
not afraid to "fail quickly." If an idea does not generate an interested
group to pray about it, then we move on not with any sense that the
idea was "bad" but rather that the time for the idea was not "good."
The result is that, conversely, when an idea does generate a sizeable
number of folks to consider its creation, there is higher energy around
that discerning season.*

*The second achievement is that there is a sense of accomplishment
in doing fewer things well rather than doing many things merely
for the sake of appearing busy. The result is that we no longer expect
that an idea will be launched into perpetuity but rather we expect
it to have a season, the end of which will open the space for the next
idea. But the most significant benefit is that, because of the personal*

investment of the parishioners, I am able to exercise my ministry in such a way that when God calls me away from this place, the core work that we have done together will enable the congregation to continue its work without needing my participation to drive it. I am free to be an advocate and a facilitator, which is a ministry model that many of my colleagues have never enjoyed.

Finally, by virtue of its focus on intentionality, a deliberative model of discernment in ministry resists obfuscation and deceit, building trust instead. In too many congregations, efficiency-driven models of clergy leadership have fostered deceit and secrets. This insufficient trust level creates doubt and insincerity in parishioners as well, as they doubt one another's motivations and loyalties. The mindful church model is able to highlight genuine transparency as not only essential to the process but also as an affirmation of the work of the Holy Spirit, focusing human energies toward glorifying God.

As a priest, I know that my relationship with Stuart is enviable. I am unapologetically happy to the core of my being to enter this season of my vocation as his partner in ministry, and the joy I experience in this role fuels all that I do.

Spiritual Imagination and a Capital Campaign

After the first three years of shared ministry, the momentum around an imaginative embodiment of mission continued with a new phase of our shared life. We realized that we are on the verge of celebrating Grace's bicentennial in 2028. The vestry worked hard to manage the finances well, and we were soon debt-free. This debt-free position enabled us to step even more fully into a new stage of community-oriented discernment and prayer as we wondered what God was leading us to explore as a spiritual community. Given this space to pray and reflect, our new guiding question became "Who is God inviting us to be as a community in our third century of shared ministry and prayer?"

All five clusters with their staff, vestry, and committee leadership stepped into this expanded space of mindful discernment. After meeting with the bishop and consulting various diocesan leaders, we committed ourselves to beginning a formal bicentennial vision process that allowed ten years for deep listening, prayer, discernment, and planning. When I asked the leadership how we could take advantage of this opportunity, the conversation immediately focused on our prior experience with the listening circles in 2014. What if there was a way to expand this experience of conversation and discernment even wider throughout the community? What if we engaged in a conversation that was grounded in "present-moment awareness" and "non-egoistic alertness"?[4]

Working in consultation with the wardens, vestry, and key staff persons, I called together a diverse committee of twelve individuals, chaired by my first senior warden, Kathy Gosselin. The men and women on the Bicentennial Vision Committee spanned seven decades and represented the full spectrum of the parish's life and ministry. We realized quickly that the vestry alone was not able to contain the full breadth and weight of the conversations, and having the vestry take sole responsibility for this task would risk a loss of institutional memory, especially given the annual turnover the vestry experiences in the election process. By having this group of twelve commit themselves to listening to these wide-ranging conversations, they could then work alongside the vestry to ensure that adequate attention is paid to the discernment process.

The Bicentennial Vision Committee immediately recognized the potential they had to continue the work of the listening circles, whose mindful conversation and prayer had been so formative in the parish's life. They recognized that a ten-year commitment was a heavy burden for anyone to bear, so they committed themselves to a two-year process of listening and gathering insight in conversations. After this two-year listening and discernment period, the bicentennial vision process shifted its focus toward embodiment, wondering how the Spirit may be guiding us to act, given what we have discerned as a community.

In this initial phase of listening and prayer, the committee focused on ways to invite conversation. We sent out a survey to the entire parish with only one statement centered on our common life as a Christian community: "As a member of the Christian community of Grace Episcopal Church, I value . . ." We invited parishioners to complete the statement after reflecting on what we value most as we live into that identity. Every member of the parish from sixth grade onward sent in five responses that were gathered and used to form a word cloud, a visual representation of our common discernment. The most commonly used words or phrases were larger in the image, focusing our attention as we pondered where the Spirit is at work in our midst.

Rather than rely only on this survey, the Bicentennial Vision Committee also made a list of every ministry group in the community— quite a lengthy list! From knitting groups to homeless ministry to finance to the Altar Guild, the committee divided itself up and scheduled visits to every single ministry group in the parish. In their conversations, the committee recognized the importance of listening first, so the initial task of their first visit was simply to be present and listen deeply, writing down the words or images that caught their hearts. In a follow-up visit to the group, they invited them to consider in a contemplative spirit where God seems to be at work through their particular ministry experience. In a flash of insight, the committee asked its fifteen-year-old member, a young woman full of joy, to be the liaison to the Finance Committee, an experience that was beautiful and profound!

We learned a great deal from our initial experience with listening circles, and we realized that we could, in essence, form a mobile listening circle of committee members who gave of themselves and journeyed out into the community in a spirit of love and curiosity. Through this extraordinary group of dedicated people, we consciously sought to root our entire vision process in an awareness of God's "wanting-to-be in our lives"[5] rather than in our own ambition and ideas.

By centering ourselves in this way, being mindful of our call to "grow into the full stature of Christ" and participate in God's mission in our world, Grace Church made an extraordinary commitment. Our imaginative reorganization slowed down the decision-making process, yet the decisions that have been made are ones that come from the heart of the entire parish—a heart that seeks to ground itself in the presence of Christ. It is not an easy process. However, it is one that we hope bears much fruit in the future. It is an experiment, if you will, of willingness, of yielding to God's call on our lives.

Underneath it all, what dynamics, theologically, are at work in our community? How can we better articulate our own formative process as a parish? What language and images can we use that may help us gain some insight to the Spirit's work among us and our participation with it? It is to this task of theological reflection that I now turn.

2
Discernment and Imagination

*It is at the level of imagination that the fateful
issues of our new world-experience must first be
mastered. It is here that culture and history are
broken, and here that the church is polarized. Old
words do not reach across the new gulfs, and it
is only in vision and oracle that we can chart the
unknown and new-name the creatures.*

*Before the message, there must be the vision,
before the sermon the hymn, before the prose the
poem.*

*Before any new theologies however secular and
radical there must be a contemporary theopoetic.
The structures of faith and confession have always
rested in hierophanies and images. But in each
new age and climate the theopoetic of the church
is reshaped in inseparable relation to the general
imagination of the time.*

—**Amos Wilder**, *Theopoetic: Theology and
Religious Imagination*

In his insightful work *Theopoetic: Theology and Religious Imagination*, the biblical scholar Amos Wilder argues that the church can
adequately confront the challenges of our current day only by a deeper

engagement with the more imaginative elements of Christian practice. Leaders in the church today, whether ordained or lay, find themselves facing immense pressure from our consumeristic and hyperindividualistic society. As the data from the Pew Forum on Religion and Public Life consistently shows, participation in organized church activities is declining. It is easy to become anxious every time this data is published, yet the data itself holds intriguing insights. Given the leadership pressures we face, we may find ourselves asking how could we possibly organize our life so that we might experience growth and renewal? How can we more fully embody our identity as the Body of Christ and thus live into our baptismal vocation "to grow into the full stature of Christ"?

The Pew Forum on Religion & Public Life data itself can be quite helpful. Even though the percentage of individuals who describe themselves as having no religious affiliation—the "nones"—has increased relative to the population as a whole, within this nones group a continued spiritual yearning remains evident. In data from the last decade, fully two-thirds (68 percent) say they believe in God and one in five (21 percent) say they pray each day.[1] Thus the category of "spiritual but not religious" that we hear so often in descriptions of contemporary church dynamics is quite complex. We cannot simply conflate church attendance with one's propensity toward spiritual and religious practice. More attention must be paid to the dynamics within this population demographic, and the assumptions of the institutional church may be enormously challenged.

To be sure, there are societal pressures that affect the church's approach to mission and ministry, yet the fault does not lie only with the external pressures. In his foreword to L. Callid Keefe-Perry's *Way to Water: A Theopoetics Primer*, the theologian Terry Veling quotes Abraham Heschel, as Heschel calls the religious institution itself to account:

It is customary to blame secular science and anti-religious philosophy for the eclipse of religion in modern society. It would be more honest to blame religion for its own defeats. Religion declined not because it was refuted, but because it became irrelevant, dull, oppressive, insipid. When faith is completely replaced by creed, worship by discipline, love by habit; when faith becomes an heirloom rather than a living fountain; when religion speaks only in the name of authority rather than with the voice of compassion—its message is meaningless.[2]

Hence, the church itself can neglect (many would argue it has indeed neglected) the deeper currents of its own potential, thus exacerbating the frustration and anxiety we experience. It is far too easy to fall prey to the pressures and anxieties of perceived decline, and church leaders quickly attach themselves to what the leadership expert Ronald Heifetz would call "technical fixes" in times of stress and strain.[3]

In my own context at Grace Church, it was tempting to rely on prepackaged leadership modules that might help guide our conversation rather than grounding such contemporary discussions in the wisdom of Christian practice and prayer. Given the anxieties we faced as a community, the hopes carried by so many people to step into a space of growth, and the expectation for something new and exciting, I, like many other pastors, felt enormous pressure to "succeed." Given this common hope for success, leaders often turn to techniques and tactics, and there are many such tools produced by publishing companies seeking to address the concerns and pressures felt by churches and religious institutions. Such products may be helpful in many regards, yet as Wilder suggests, "All recipes and programmed strategies fall short of accounting for the full mystery of language where deep calls to deep."[4]

Given the complexity within the Pew Forum polls and other venues, we would do well to pay attention to the persistent yearning found within so many people in our world. When we dig deeper into the data itself, we may find that there are ample grounds for hope within a more prayerful approach that engages the spiritual imagination of the tradition. In a prescient observation, Wilder notes that in the face of our hyperindividualistic behaviors and our consumer-obsessed culture, such a deeper dimension often rises to the surface:

> The more our scientific technoculture ripens the more it seems to call forth, as a kind of shadow, a mentality compounded of magic and mythology. But this new climate reminds the church of its own deeper dream and here we have the intramural aspect. What forms will a theopoetic take today which will both quicken the tradition and at the same time speak to the general imagination of the age?[5]

The pressures are both external and internal in origin. For those of us within the Christian tradition, we find ourselves with a rich opportunity for insight and renewal—even as we experience institutional resistance and suspicion of any perceived threat to the status quo. Given the challenges we face, we could indeed reflect more intently on how we understand our common life through the lens of God's dynamic and triune nature rather than persist in rigid patterns of behavior. As L. Callid Keefe-Perry cautions us, "I believe that if Christians accept the articulation and explanations of God that have come before simply *because* they have come before, then what is being practiced is not some kind of reverence for tradition, but a form of idolatrous traditionalism."[6]

The greatest challenge within the breadth of the Christian tradition is not a loss of membership or a rapid decrease in budgets or a loss of prestige or cultural sway. Rather, our greatest danger rests with a loss of spiritual imagination and the willingness to cultivate a practice of faith that harnesses the potential within our own religious tradition. When we neglect our more substantive identity and are driven instead by superficial notions of success, the Christian community becomes starved of the more profound hope found within the gospels. The failure to cultivate our imaginative capacity greatly impedes leadership development and religious practices within all our religious communities.

A Prophetic Word

As frustrating as it is for us, this struggle is nothing new to religious communities. The Hebrew prophets faced their own challenges centuries ago as they faced the pressures of outside powers on one hand and the complacency of the religious institution on the other. The prophet Jeremiah is a striking example of creative faithfulness: he can imagine God's saving presence even in the face of potential annihilation. The temple cult had failed to lived up to its own call to trust wholly in God's presence, and the actions of the entire society set the entire nation on the path of defeat. However, even in the midst of such pain and anguish, Jeremiah is able to imagine hope:

> See, I am going to bring them from the land of the north,
> and gather them from the farthest parts of the earth,
> among them the blind and the lame,
> those with child and those in labor, together;
> a great company, they shall return here.
> With weeping they shall come,
> and with consolations I will lead them back,
> I will let them walk by brooks of water,
> in a straight path in which they shall not stumble;
> for I have become a father to Israel,
> and Ephraim is my firstborn.
>
> JER. 31:8–9, NRSV

It is Jeremiah's inspired imagination that allowed the people to see what was possible, and his capacity for hope in the midst of catastrophe can encourage us to catch a glimpse of God's grace in our circumstances as well. His willingness and openness to God invited a hopeful perspective on God's actions in the world.

First Glimpses into a Possibility

In 2010 I began a two-year residency with the Shalem Institute for Spiritual Formation called *Going Deeper: Clergy Spiritual Life and Leadership*. Over the course of those two years, and after an additional year of follow-up study, I had the opportunity to share deeply meaningful conversations with Tilden Edwards, other teachers, and fellow clergy. The twelve clergy participants shared a common desire: to rest more fully in the Holy Spirit's guidance and help lead our spiritual communities from this more imaginative space of prayer and trust. We came from many traditions, including the Presbyterian Church, United Methodist Church, and the Anglican Church of New Zealand, yet we shared a common yearning to experience a more imaginative and deeper practice of spiritual leadership.

My time with Shalem was invaluable for me as I continued to discern my vocation to explore contemplative leadership models within my parish context. I did not know if what I sought was even possible. Was the only way of parish leadership one that relied heavily on the program-maintenance model? What could I learn from the richness of the contemplative tradition, and how might I be able to translate this into my parish community? As Edwards often said, "What would it look like to trust in the movement of the living Spirit?"

In many conversations in my parish and diocese, I had felt like an outlier. My clergy colleagues around me seemed to have ample management skills that I lacked, and I chafed at some of their assumptions about how to approach pastoral conflicts within their communities. It seemed there was a right answer—or a more appropriate and typical one—that I lacked.

In my conversations with Edwards and the other leaders, I came to learn that there is a direct relationship between the dynamics of an imaginative approach to ministry and our willingness to trust the movements of the Holy Spirit, the Spirit of Christ that invigorates the life of the church today. In 2010, Shalem published a short monograph, *Valuing and Nurturing a Mind-in-Heart Way*, that had originally been included in Edwards's larger work, *Embracing the Call to Spiritual Depth: Gifts for Contemplative Living.* This monograph focused specifically on the dynamics of what "the promise of a contemplatively-oriented seminary" might hold, as the subtitle indicates. It has been an invaluable resource for me as I focus my ministry here at Grace Church.

In this work, Edwards contends that enormous opportunities could come with renewed emphasis on "new ways of teaching, learning, leading, and living," leading to "deeper spiritual formation of both ordained and lay spiritual leaders."[7] This contemplatively-oriented model calls us to set aside other dominant models that may be in place, such as the predominant academic model that Edwards highlights within seminary education. As he argues, "This shift would involve a fuller appreciation of mind-in-heart contemplative awareness as a different way of knowing reality that can ground and complement the rational mind's way of knowing. Such an integration is particularly vital for perceiving spiritual reality, which involves a distinctive way of seeing and being present."[8] Edwards's challenge to the predominantly academic orientation of seminary education resonated deeply with my own struggles with the prevalent program-maintenance organizational model for parish leadership.

Reflecting on the way education and formation takes place here, Edwards asks a crucial question: "Can [these models and frameworks as they exist now] help a student touch the intrinsically mystical

ground of the faith's founders and movers through a process of rational conveyance of information and interpretation?"[9] For him, it is a
question of epistemology, in asking if the ways we currently know
and are organized are "sufficient to help student's inner openness and
digestion of that reality."[10]

The Spiritual Heart and Administration

It is not that we must neglect the crucial aspects of rational thought
and analysis, or of structured organization and strategic planning. We
must organize ourselves well, and we would do well to remember, as
the adage goes, "Good administration is good pastoral care." Yet, the
theologian Thomas Oden raises a cautionary note when it comes to
how church communities approach administration:

> Having borrowed heavily from programmatic management
> procedures while forgetting much of their traditional root-
> age, church administration has become an orphan discipline
> vaguely wondering about its true parentage.[11]

As Oden explains later in his book, we must remember that embedded within the very word *administration* is the call to a fuller appreciation of *ministry* within all members of our spiritual communities.[12]
Our rational minds and organizational schemes are useful and necessary for the function of our communities, yet our hearts are called
toward something deeper still. As Edwards reminds us,

> There is a dimension of our being where names are lost and
> communion/union is found. There in graced moments our
> whole being is drawn and tinctured with confident, reveal-
> ing, "enlightening" love. This radiant love spontaneously
> spills into our daily lives, however limited by the fractures in
> and around us that hide our true Home.[13]

Such a focus is the call to a contemplatively-oriented practice of spiritual leadership, a way of being and guiding that facilitates an engagement with the Spirit's call upon our lives. This Spirit draws us into communion not only with one another but with the Triune God in whom we encounter the interconnected and dynamic pattern for our own existence.

At the end of the monograph, after reflecting on specific challenges and opportunities within the seminary context, Edwards offers an insight that has changed my understanding of parish leadership. It is this challenge that led me to explore such a reorientation in my parish. This emphasis on a contemplative grounding is necessary in our current situation, recognizing the complexities of the social and religious environment in which we live. Edwards's argument is this:

> If such a contemplative orientation and its imaginative living out does not show itself more fully in seminaries of the future, this formational and modeling task then necessarily would fall more fully to congregations and other spiritual centers of religious/spiritual life.[14]

Given Edwards's thoughts, my response would be as follows: Why not *begin* with parish churches? Why can parishes not be the initiating ground for such an orientation that seeks more fully to trust the Spirit's guidance? This was the challenge that resonated with me, a particular vocational discernment within my own pastoral leadership.

At the root of this entire contemplative orientation of leadership and formation lies a recognition of the call to live, as Edwards and the broader contemplative tradition describe it, from our "spiritual heart": the capacity within the entire community to lean into God's presence in our lives rather than trust solely in our own strengths and agendas. The spiritual heart can be nurtured and cultivated in such a way that the entire community encounters God, provoking further reflection on what it means to trust the Spirit's guidance. Such glimpses of divine grace can become habitual, leading to "an expansive, intuitive capacity that draws us to an immediate, participative, pre-cognitive awareness of what is."[15]

A Deeper Look at Discernment

Interestingly, Edwards's work on such a contemplative orientation has strong connections with the imaginative element within Ignatian spirituality as well. The Jesuits have a long history of communal discernment for decision-making within a community of faith. Whereas Edwards describes the reality and nurturing of the "spiritual heart" within a faith community, Ignatian spirituality emphasizes the explicit presence of the Spirit in the life of the group. How is the group aware of the Spirit's guidance in their approach to making a decision?

In "Communal Discernment," George J. Schemel, SJ, and Judith A. Roemer describe the Ignatian approach to such a Spirit-oriented leadership. Echoing much of Edwards's description of a community conscious of its grounding in the Holy Spirit's guidance, as well as Amos Wilder's call to an imaginative approach to the challenges of community existence, they argue for a posture that holds "an explicit attitude and atmosphere of faith":

> Communal discernment is not another group method along with Robert's Rules, management by objectives, paternal or maternal guidance, or any other such process or structure. Discernment demands that we ask the further question: "Where is God leading me and my group in this concrete situation?" This is an important feature of communal discernment, because in discernment we are weighing and deciding among goods rather than choosing between good and evil. We are not asking how much money we can save, how much profit we can accumulate, where we can sacrifice now in order

to get ahead later. We are asking quite simply: "Where is the invitation of grace? In what choice do we find God?"[16]

When a group needs to make a decision, the object itself is not the primary focus. The experience of the community's awareness and grounding in the Spirit's guidance is of utmost importance. Whereas my own experience has been that groups too often push for a quick decision around critical issues or concerns, the Ignatian perspective resists any decision-making that may have its roots in anxiety or fear. As the authors argue,

> Part of learning to live with communal discernment is learn-
> ing to live with process. The group needs time and patience
> to work with its own real agenda and to be satisfied with the
> sometimes small, but clearer truths that surface from it.[17]

Any clarity that is gained in such a process is infused with the Spirit's guidance rather than any individual's or group's agenda. Such an experience affirms God's presence in the reality of the community as it celebrates the group's participation with God's direction. This is prayerful decision-making. As the authors explain, "Discernment rests on the belief that the human organism is made rightly, and that God actually works perceptibly in one's symbolic and affective consciousness."[18]

The reality of discernment within a community takes time. It is a process that cannot be rushed in hopes that one can "get on" to the work at hand. As Schemel and Roemer point out, any group will experience temptations to avoid the risk and vulnerability entailed in such discernment work. In reflecting on how all sides of an issue are equally discussed in a posture of prayer, they describe how a group should be cautious as it draws near to a point of decision-making: "One of the biggest temptations at this point in the communal discernment is to 'form consensus' instead of reading the consensus that is actually forming in the group."[19] I think of Kathy Gosselin's reflection on the vestry's discernment process at Grace and the way they took their time, passing the ball of yarn and listening to one another and to the Spirit. Indeed, Kathy caught a glimpse of this dynamic at work when she wrote, "And I kept alert throughout the evening's conversation in order to catch the Spirit in action, pointing it out as subtly as I could."

I also think of the importance of knowing what the logistical boundaries are within any judicatory, diocesan, or parochial framework. In my own situation, there are clear delineations as to where much formal authority lies, and it is helpful to make sure there is clarity in this regard that can, in reality, decrease a great deal of anxiety. That being said, we shouldn't remain so focused on those formal descriptions of authority that we lose sight of the constant invitation to collaboration and a more vulnerable sharing of stories, hopes, and dreams. As the rector or head of staff of my parish, I may be accountable for many aspects of our common life. However, as a priest, I am responsible for fostering a prayerful engagement of mutual collaboration of the parish with regards to our shared ministry.

The discernment process is much more about gaining an awareness of the Spirit's guidance in a community's life than it is about the community taking initiative to succeed in making a decision. We participate with God, and we are called into a relationship through which and in which we grow in our awareness of the Spirit of Christ at the heart of our own being. As Tilden Edwards notes,

> Thus, what's important is not the search for some particular experience but bringing to every moment a simple desire to be present to Reality as it is in God, or to put it more personally, present for the divine Beloved through whatever happens.[20]

Perhaps it is only through yielding a sense of control that one can step more fully into this space of discernment. This is what Edwards describes as "relinquishing a sense of self-centered control of life as a larger identity in living radiant Love emerges."[21]

So, we are left with the challenge to engage in a different way of being, a fresh way of relating to one another and practicing our faith within community. We cannot deny the pressures we face in our myriad ministry contexts. The challenges of numerical decline can be frustrating and disheartening, yet we have an opportunity to trust more explicitly in the Holy Spirit's call on our lives. In the catechism of the Book of Common Prayer, we are asked "What is the Christian hope?" The answer is simultaneously challenging and reassuring:

> The Christian hope is to live with confidence in newness and fullness of life, and to await the coming of Christ in glory, and the completion of God's purpose for the world. (BCP, 861)

The juxtaposition of "confidence" and "newness and fullness of life" is indeed the invitation to a faith grounded in discernment and imagination. It is a practice of faith that takes seriously God's action in our lives, becoming ever more aware of our identity and vocation. We seek to embody hope here and now—even as we pray for that hope to be fully consummated.

All this being said, how can we become more aware of the reality of this hope? What images or insights might we explore that could enliven our imaginative engagement with our practice of faith? It is on this question of increased awareness that I seek to focus in the next chapter.

3
Mindfulness and Conversion

The Sutra of Mindfulness says, "When walking, the practitioner must be conscious that he is walking. When sitting, the practitioner must be conscious that he is sitting. When lying down, the practitioner must be conscious that he is lying down. . . . No matter what position one's body is in, the practitioner must be conscious of that position. Practicing thus, the practitioner lives in direct and constant mindfulness of the body." The mindfulness of one's body is not enough, however. We must be conscious of each breath, each movement, every thought and feeling, everything which has any relation to ourselves.

—**Thich Nhat Hanh**, *The Miracle of Mindfulness*

The first time I ever met a Buddhist monk, I was visiting the University of Central Arkansas in Conway, Arkansas. I was part of a small group of students from Lyon College who drove there to experience the richness of the religious practice of a group of Tibetan Buddhist monks from, of all places, Georgia. We had the opportunity to explore this exotic tradition that we had learned so much about in our Introduction to Religion class. We had read about meditation and mindfulness practice, and we now had the opportunity to see it firsthand—and to share in the practice ourselves.

The monks began the session with a chant unlike any I had ever heard. The deep sonorous tones—with each monk chanting a three-note chord—filled the space and helped me relax. As we sat there in the auditorium, a senior monk invited us to sit with our backs against the chair. With our feet flat on the floor and our hands lying gently on our legs, we closed our eyes and began paying attention to our breath. I did not remember having ever paid attention to my breathing in that way, to focus gently when I inhaled and exhaled. We sat there for what seemed like an eternity, gently breathing in and out, learning how to focus our attention on this seemingly simple practice. The monk was teaching us how to notice life in a way I had never before experienced.

It did not take long before a thought came swirling into my consciousness, and the gate that then opened allowed in a flood of thoughts that shattered the focus I had only glimpsed. But, the monk said, this was normal. We are human. We think and we become distracted by all the details of life that surrounds us. Rather than becoming angry at losing focus, he advised us simply to notice that we are thinking and see what happens when we pay attention to the distraction itself. He guided us into a posture whereby we gently acknowledged the distracting thought and then, in his words, released it. We brought our attention back to our breath, that constant teacher and tool that is always present with us. By doing this, he taught us, we were learning what it meant to be truly aware rather than reactive to whatever surrounds us at the moment. By not grasping the thought as it rose in our consciousness, we could return our attention to the more nuanced reality of existence.

My day there at the university was my first taste of a practice that fostered much growth in my spiritual life. I continued my relationship with Tibetan Buddhism as well as with various Zen teachers with whom I came into contact since then. Throughout my seminary studies, I noticed that more and more people were finding something meaningful in mindfulness practice. There seemed to be an interest in the basic teachings of mindfulness that resonated with many people in a range of life circumstances—including longtime pastors in various Christian denominations. When the Dalai Lama came to visit Atlanta three times over the course of ten years, I would often meet colleagues at Emory University and other venues who had traveled to hear His Holiness speak about the importance of paying attention.

When I was a newly ordained priest, I would take over twenty of my parishioners to a local Tibetan Buddhist Center to study on Tuesday evenings with the monks there, alongside students from Barbara Brown Taylor's religion class at Piedmont College. Barbara and I would sit in the back and observe how an interest in mindfulness practice could support students of all sorts in deepening their explorations in their own spiritual lives. On some nights, there were more Episcopalians than Buddhists in that room, something that intrigues me still. Also, it should come as no surprise that this particular center, Drepung Loseling Monastery, is the actual home of the monks whom I met years prior in Arkansas. The Spirit does indeed blow where she will.

Mindfulness Saturation

Mindfulness practice has saturated our culture. There are classes on mindful eating, mindful parenting, mindful workplaces, and any other variation on the theme one can imagine. Mindfulness practice is offered by many Fortune 500 companies and other businesses, and has now gone mainstream in the culture. In his insightful work *Mindful America: The Mutual Transformation of Buddhist Meditation and American Culture*, the religion scholar Jeff Wilson describes the phenomenon of mindfulness and the complex effect the growth of this particular spiritual practice has had within American society. Wilson tracks the evolution of mindfulness as it has spread throughout our nation. There have been pivotal moments, he argues, such as when Bill Moyers featured Jon Kabat-Zinn's Mindfulness-Based Stress

Reduction on the 1993 PBS special *Healing and the Mind*, which helped broaden the appeal of the practice. This increased awareness spurred further engagement with Kabat-Zinn's work, leading to the foundation of the Duke Center for Integrative Medicine in 1998.[1] With the increased visibility of the practice, more books were published, more public teachings were offered, and the practice became more and more popular.

Interestingly, Wilson notes the way mindfulness practice has been medicalized, mainstreamed, marketed, and moralized within American society. Specifically noting the way that American consumer culture is focused on health, youth, and vitality, Wilson describes the dynamic of medicalization as follows:

> Being able to approach mindfulness as a technique of personal spirituality and also having the option of seeing it as a biological or psychological process related to health and science extends the possibilities for mindfulness in America, providing familiar access points to most of the population regardless of their individual religious or secular backgrounds. Medicalization specifically grants mindfulness access to many new sites otherwise off-limits for mere spirituality, such as hospitals, schools, and other places where secular culture tends to set the terms of acceptable discussion and practice.[2]

While one should be cautious of any spiritual practice that is "used" solely to increase one's prosperity or success, it is important to avoid dismissing the depth of mindfulness practice out of hand. As Wilson says, "The mindfulness movement *is*, and because it is, we must each grapple with its manifestations and draw our conclusions."[3] Perhaps mindfulness as a spiritual practice is undergoing the same pressures from a consumerist American culture to which all other faith practices have been subjected. What is clear is that there is *something* in American culture today to which mindfulness practice speaks.

When we reflect intently on the practice, authentic mindfulness can be a profound spiritual tool for one's life. As Bhante Gunaratana describes,

> Mindfulness practice is the practice of being 100 percent honest with ourselves. When we watch our own minds and body, we notice certain things that are unpleasant to realize. Since we do not like them, we try to reject them. . . . If we are mindful, we will diligently use our wisdom to look into our own mind.[4]

It is a discipline of focused reflection in which all the distractions and preoccupations of our lives are laid bare. Through observation, we are invited to be honest with ourselves and also compassionate with ourselves. We are encouraged to persevere in the practice by continually bringing our awareness back to a space of greater freedom and peace.

One of the most ancient mindfulness practices within the Buddhist tradition is vipassana. This core technique is one of the most readily adapted or translated into our Western world, known to many as "insight meditation."[5] In Pali, a language native to India and Buddhism's most sacred language, insight meditation is known as *vipassana bhavana*. The word *bhavana* comes from the root word *bhu*, which itself means "to grow or to become." The image is one of cultivation and growth; and the word itself, according to Gunaratana, is used only in relation to the mind.[6] The word *vipassana* itself is made up of two root words: *passana*, meaning "seeing or perceiving"; and *vi* meaning "into and through a special way."[7] By placing all these etymological understandings together, Gunaratana explains that

> the whole meaning of the word *vipassana* is looking into something with clarity and precision, seeing each component as distinct, and piercing all the way through to perceive the

most fundamental reality of that thing. This process leads to insight into the basic reality of whatever is being examined. Put these words together and *vipassana bhavana* means the cultivation of the mind toward the aim of seeing in a special way that leads to insight and full understanding.[8]

Even in this short reflection on the purpose and origin of mindfulness practice, one can begin to see the appeal it would have in a culture bombarded by so many distractions and pressures. How can we see more clearly? How can we perceive what is true underneath the complexities of our lives?

A Meeting of Christianity and Buddhism

Within the broader Christian contemplative tradition, one encounters many conversations between Christian mystics and theologians and Buddhist monks and practitioners. The writings of Thomas Keating, John Main, Laurence Freeman, Martin Laird, Basil Pennington, Cynthia Bourgeault, Richard Rohr, Tilden Edwards, and James Finley, as well as phenomena such as the Centering Prayer movement or the World Community for Christian Meditation all testify to a common passion for a deeper awareness. Many see Thomas Merton's visit to His Holiness the Dalai Lama in 1968 as a watershed moment in Christian-Buddhist relations. Merton's interest in Buddhist philosophy and practice, while challenged by many at the time, has influenced many Christian contemplatives in the decades since. Indeed, it is evident that the impact was mutual, since the Dalai Lama and several Buddhist monks came to the Abbey of Gethsemani in Kentucky in 1996 to continue studying the rich connections between Christian contemplative prayer and Buddhist meditation.

While recognizing that connections do exist, Gunaratana nevertheless draws a distinction between the practice of mindfulness and the understanding of prayer and contemplation in both the Jewish and Christian traditions. As he observes,

> Within the Judeo-Christian tradition [*sic*] we find two over-lapping practices called prayer and contemplation. Prayer is a direct address to a spiritual entity. Contemplation is a prolonged period of conscious thought about a specific topic, usually a religious ideal or scriptural passage. From the standpoint of mental cultivation, both of these activities are exercises in concentration. The normal deluge of conscious thought is restricted, and the mind is brought to one conscious area of operation. The results are those you find in any concentrative practice: deep calm, a physiological slowing of the metabolism, and a sense of peace and well-being.[9]

For Gunaratana, Buddhism's understanding of mindfulness, an exercise cultivating awareness, has qualities distinct from those found in both Jewish and Christian frameworks, even while it bears some resemblances to it. As he argues, "Within the Buddhist tradition, concentration is also highly valued. But a new element is added and more highly stressed: the element of awareness."[10] For Buddhists, the goal or aim is to transcend conscious thought, a concept that persists on the level of the illusory image of a distinct self. Through the cultivation of vipassana practice, Gunaratana notes, "We learn to listen to our own thoughts without being caught up in them."[11]

While Gunaratana draws such a distinction between how he understands prayer and contemplation in the Jewish and Christian traditions and the richness of developing awareness within vipassana, significant resonances between the traditions remain. Indeed, within the Christian contemplative tradition we can discover a depth of experience that questions Gunaratana's hard-and-fast distinction altogether. Consider how Tilden Edwards describes the contemplative mind:

Within us there is a capacity for touching reality more directly than the thinking mind. It is activated when we're willing to let go of the thoughts that come through our mind and to sit in the spacious openness that appears between and behind them.[12]

For Gunaratana, the overarching concern is the persistence of the thinking function to guide and direct a person's life. When our thoughts frame our existence and shape the way we understand and seek to control reality, we continue to fall prey to self-delusions and pride. Tilden Edwards would wholeheartedly agree. As Edwards contends, "When the thinking mind comes into play to interpret that reality through its categories and conditioning, and with the influence of our ego desires for security in that interpretation," our "pure contemplative awareness" is shattered.[13]

Edwards argues that the potential for such an awareness is a gift of the Holy Spirit that rests within each person and draws us into a fuller communion with the Triune God: "We each touch the same substantive reality there."[14] Each person has such a "capacity for intuitive direct awareness" in their life, and it shapes the way they come to understand the nature of community, "because we find everyone and everything present and interrelated."[15] His description of this space is illuminating:

If you haven't done that before, then when you do you're in for a major discovery. It will be like finding a door that you didn't even know existed. As that door opens, you are led into the reality before you much more directly than your thinking mind can do. Eventually you may find yourself intimately present *within* whatever you see. You are part of it. You know it as it is, just as when you were a small child and your open mind directly entered what you saw and remained there longer than in later years, when your trained interpretive mind quickly took over what you saw on its own terms.[16]

Here, Edwards's words strikingly echo those of Gunaratana, when Gunaratana describes our struggle to maintain such a degree of awareness.

It is crucial to point out that such a focused practice of developing a greater awareness of the phenomena of existence has deep Christian roots. This is not an exercise or tool restricted solely to a Buddhist-Hindu worldview or religious ethos. Accounts of gaining a greater awareness or insight can be found embedded within the more ancient Christian tradition. When we explore our scriptural texts with an eye to such occasions of insight, we notice the reorienting experience of Jacob's dream (Genesis 28), Elijah's experience of the profound mystery of God while hiding in the cave (1 Kings 19), and Saul's experience of the overpowering brightness of Christ's presence while on the road to Damascus (Acts 9). Indeed, there may be no better biblical description of the potential insights of mindfulness within the Jewish and Christian traditions than Jacob's attestation upon waking from his dream: "Surely the LORD is in this place—and I did not know it!" (Gen. 28:16).

My own study and experience of mindfulness practice, and my personal acquaintance with many others who find it helpful, leads me to affirm Amos Wilder's contention that "a creative theopoetic is called for, therefore, not only to vitalize a traditional theology but also to relate our Christian experience to the new sensibility of our time and its images and cults."[17] Given the complexities, stresses, and expectations of our cultural context, and given the continued yearning for a greater experience of God's presence, might mindfulness practice offer a "door," as Edwards puts it, for Christian communities to delve more deeply into their own practice and shared discipleship?

Give Us Eyes to See More Clearly

As we continue to seek a greater awareness of God's presence, reflection on mindfulness practice might help enormously. When we try to cultivate a greater awareness, it behooves us to spend some time wondering how we do, in fact, perceive the world around us. To restate an earlier question: How can we see more clearly? How might our spiritual imaginations be stretched or expanded as we engage in the world around us?

In the early months of my time at Grace Church, when we were involved in four months of what we called listening circles, we sought to engage in a conversation around vision and insight. I wanted to learn from those participating about their most formative moments in the parish. I also wanted to take the first steps in discovering where we were being led as a parish. To gain this insight, I needed to frame the question very carefully.

I remembered the detailed work done by Courtney Cowart and Jim Goodmann of the Society for the Increase of the Ministry when they had come to my previous parish, St. Benedict's in Smyrna, Georgia.[18] The rector, Brian Sullivan, and I had invited them to help our vestry and staff with vocational discernment. We wondered how we might initiate a conversation about shared ministry and discipleship. Cowart and Goodmann spent a long time with us as we framed specific story prompts. We learned that the questions you ask are vital in cultivating a truly reflective and formative space.

As we began the listening circles at Grace Church, I chose the framework of *mindfulness* in the hope that the associated images and connotations might assist us in exploring vision and growth. I had central questions in mind: How can we see the history of this community more clearly? How might we see the Spirit at work, leading us into a new place of spiritual maturity and enhanced community? What resistances might we see within the community that could, in themselves, offer opportunities for engagement and growth? I knew that in group conversations such as this, some people would take the opportunity to complain about what they did not like. Others would vent about problems or decisions that had made them angry. Still others might dredge up old wounds, hoping to reframe the narrative by reminding those gathered of pain and frustration. Our time together was, indeed, an experience of mindfulness. It was an experiment in sharing from our spiritual hearts rather than from our agendas and thinking minds alone. It was a space of risk and potential insight.

By framing the question around *meaning*, I hoped we would plunge into a more focused awareness and reflection rather than remain on the surface level of venting and agendas. I hoped that a question grounded in meaning might facilitate a conversation that would embrace risk and honor the experiences of each person in the room. I also hoped that a reflection on meaning might connect to the probing work of the Holy Spirit, assisting those gathered to wonder about how the presence of Christ might be at work in the life of this community. When, for instance, someone might report a frustrating experience, we found that by asking how that experience was *meaningful*, the memory of the experience could be reframed. The question about meaning had the potential to cultivate a greater self-awareness as well as the perception of the Spirit of Christ at work within. By entering prayerfully into this shared space, we sought to experience something of what St. Paul prayed for the Church in Ephesus:

> I pray that the God of our Lord Jesus Christ, the Father of glory, may give you a spirit of wisdom and revelation as you come to know him, so that, with the eyes of your heart enlightened, you may know what is the hope to which he has called you, what are the riches of his glorious inheritance among the saints, and what is the immeasurable greatness of his power for us who believe, according to the working of his great power. (Eph. 1:17–19)

We sought to have the "eyes of our hearts enlightened" by the Holy Spirit as we took the risk of such a mindful leadership.

As Tilden Edwards contends, "Contemplative awareness needs to begin on the personal level."[19] Through the sharing of such prayer-grounded conversations, new insights can be gained in the life of the entire community. Edwards's reflection is apt:

> Spiritual awakening is never for us alone. The Spirit shows itself to be a very public as well as personal face of God. What happens to us, like an energized wave drawn to the shore, is meant to refresh and reshape the shore as needed. We bring what's been given to us into the situations of our lives—in this case, the congregation—and what's been given to us interacts with what's been given to others. That interaction, pervaded by the Spirit's presence, leavens decisions in meetings, the expression of our liturgies and homilies, education, mission projects, and the rest of the life of the church.[20]

Thus the entire community can share in such an awakening through prayer and attentive listening. In such an exercise, our perception of God's presence can widen and lead us into an even greater awareness of our identity as the Body of Christ. Of course, mindfulness, in and of itself, is not the goal or aim within Christian practice. We do not seek awareness just to be aware; rather, for Christians, we pray that we may be illumined by the Holy Spirit so that we may live more deeply in tune with God's living presence in the world.

Conversion and Illumination

The theological images of *conversion* and *illumination* might be the most appropriate descriptors of the Christian mindfulness that we are suggesting. In these moments of greater awareness and insight, we are offered clarity in the midst of the pressures and complexities of our lives, especially in these days of pandemic uncertainty, potential healing of racial injustice, and ecological negligence.

Robert Hughes, a retired professor from the School of Theology at the University of the South, speaks to this movement from self-focus to a more Spirit-focused awareness in *Beloved Dust: Tides of the Spirit in the Christian Life*. At one point he describes the common experience of being stuck in a cycle of disillusionment and resentment, born of a sense of entitlement combined with unrealistic expectations of life, others, and even oneself. His picture of the inner state of one riddled with disillusionment is apt:

> Finally, when I grow weary of [resentment], I end up in resignation, seeming to accept life in a kind of bitter and cynical skepticism I call realistic but which has as its essence a giant middle finger raised into the heart of the cosmos. Unless something makes me notice, I shall go bumping down these stairs every time on a kind of automatic pilot.[21]

Such a sense of being on autopilot is pervasive in our world today, a state that Walter Brueggemann often described as "psychic numbness."[22]

Hughes describes the conversion that is needed in such a state of existence. He recognizes that the dynamic of conversion has two components: what he calls "conversion from" and "conversion to." This "whole package of conversion" is *metanoia*, or repentance. It is summed up in the double movement of change found in the preaching of both John the Baptist and Jesus: "The time is fulfilled, and the kingdom of God has come near; repent, and believe the good news" (Mark 1:15). In conversion, as Hughes explains, we *turn away* from the illusion or distraction when we *turn toward* the fulfillment or promise. As he says, "We are able to see what we turn from in its true colors, and really for the first time, only because another possibility has appeared that gives us something to turn *toward*."[23] This experience, as Hughes describes it, is one of judgment; however, it is a judgment that is life-giving rather than terrifying or damning. His vivid image of waking up presents the role of judgment within conversion as an invitation to develop greater awareness and thus live more deliberately: "Judgment is not so much designed to get us to be good from fear of punishment as it is a wake-up call. "Wake up! Smell the coffee! Get a life."[24]

One is again reminded of the stories of Jacob, Elijah, and Saul, among others. These pivotal figures in both the Jewish and Christian traditions struggled and resisted in different ways, asserting themselves and their own plans rather than God's. In all three accounts, God took the initiative and reoriented the way they understood their lives, purpose, and potential. The greater awareness they received—the insight they experienced—was a gift of the Spirit that reconfigured their existence. Hughes would argue that each of them experienced a profound conversion.

Conversion is experienced within the particular, unique circumstances of a person or a community's life. There is not one form or pattern of conversion that a community can package and market; indeed, conversion is not a facile technique that can be taught to someone else. As Hughes states, "What is important is not so much the medium by which the call is conveyed as the recognition that the Holy Spirit is operating in all of the various media."[25] The Holy Spirit empowers the conversion experience that makes possible the insight of grace. The resistances we experience within ourselves and within a community are very real. Therefore, much of parish ministry focuses on ways to become more aware of these resistances as well as the Spirit's invitations.

Resistance and Insight: A Personal Story

Recently I asked a prior senior warden and current chancellor for our parish, Jason Voyles, to describe his experience at Grace Church, paying close attention to areas where he has encountered the transition, or turning, from resistance to greater insight.

*I remember sitting down at a table for the first "listening session"
Stuart hosted on a Wednesday evening shortly after officially beginning his tenure as rector of Grace Church. The church was still in
its "honeymoon" phase with our new rector, but given the experience
many in the parish had gone through, many were apprehensive about
when this phase would end and things would "return to normal."
Interestingly, I think that most of the people attending expected to
have Stuart stand up and tell them his plans for the parish: what
direction we should head, how we should get there, and what role
each of us would play. Stuart turned this completely on its head. He
invited everyone to share their dreams and use their imaginations
to discern what Grace Church could be. His invitation was not to
continue doing things because "we've always done it that way" but
instead to be contemplative about our life as a parish and what this
life could be for everyone.*

*This imagining mindset has been a shift, and it has sometimes
been somewhat difficult. At first I saw resistance in areas where
parishioners felt as though they had carved out their niche and were
content. "Why were we trying to come in and change everything?"
they wondered. To many, things were working fine and there was no
need to try to "redefine" what the parish was. It was a balancing act
to try to reassure parishioners that the church was still their church
home. Many parishioners feared being cast aside as they saw a new
wave of volunteers that would come in and supplant them. This has
created some friction between the old guard and the new recruits and
I'm sure has led to our clergy having many long conversations with
parishioners, but this has ended up being a positive development in
the long run. It has allowed many in the parish to have long-overdue
discussions, and it has allowed some healing and catharsis for many
in the parish.*

*Once the idea of mindfulness began to take root, it was amazing to
see the transformation in the parish. One could almost feel the energy*

in the air. It was an immense positive force emanating from the parish. People were invited to dream and to imagine and you could see it in their eyes when discussing the church's future. The hope and sense of childlike wonder was palpable. It seemed that for the first time in a long time parishioners really felt that they had a voice in (and a stake in) the future of the parish. They felt that their input was desired and meaningful. And, to be quite honest, it has been very much so. The idea of being mindful about the church and its future has tapped into resources within parishioners that I had no idea existed.

As the parish has become more accustomed to contemplating our shared life together, the circle of our parish has been drawn wider. Again, what I think of as the typical church paradigm has been turned on its head. Rather than invite people to attend service on Sunday and then hope that they decide to get involved in the broader life of the church, this shared mindfulness has allowed people to imagine their space within the life of the church and truly find their home in the parish. This has resulted in a marked increase in attendance on Sunday and revitalization of the church's ministries. As people have become more mindful about their place in the church and the future of the church, they have become more invested in the life of the parish. I now see people are genuinely excited about the prospect of attending church, rather than attending out of some sense of obligation.

This isn't to say that Grace Church won't have its share of challenges in the future. However, in practicing mindfulness, I feel that the parish as a whole is training to be able to handle any trials and tribulations that may arise. Rather than having an attitude of gloom and inevitability of some negative occurrence, I see the parish meeting its challenges with enthusiasm and daring to do the hard work of being mindful about where the church's future lies.

Voyles's personal testimony supports Hughes's contention that the experience of conversion, entailing as it does both reorientation and risk, opens the possibility of receiving greater insight and clarity. We do not so much *gain* insight and awareness as we *receive* it and participate in it, and this light that we encounter in these moments of mindfulness empower us to delve even more deeply into our practice of prayer.

These graces of illumination inspire and encourage us onward as a community. We realize that our limitations do not have to define us; rather, God's love beckons us forward into new territory. We learn to resist yielding to fear and anxiety, as pervasive as they may be. We come to see our true identity in Christ, the One who was transfigured before his disciples as an embodiment of God's grace and who calls us to greater participation in the divine life itself. Jesus's moment of illumination reveals what we are to become. This true self finds its full expression, of course, in our baptismal identity and the experience of our transfigured and sacramental life in Christ, and it is to this area that I now wish to turn.

4
Transfiguration and Illumination

*In the strength of that glimpse, things become
possible. We can confront today's business
with new thoughts and feelings, reflect on our
sufferings and our failures with some degree
of hope—not with a nice and easy message of
consolation but with the knowledge that there is a
depth to the world's reality and out of that comes
the light which will somehow connect, around
and in Jesus Christ, all the complex, painful,
shapeless experience of human beings.*

—**Rowan Williams**, "The Transfiguration"

In the previous chapters I argued that a particularly Christian understanding of mindfulness practice can be an imaginative invitation for
ministry, given the myriad challenges of contemporary parish discussions around leadership development and discipleship. Harkening
back to Amos Wilder's challenge to explore a "contemporary theopoetic," I have looked toward the modern phenomena of mindfulness practice in a way that offers meaningful opportunities for any
who practice the Christian faith. The challenges the church faces
are quite real, and we have ample theological and spiritual resources
within the broader Christian tradition that can offer hope amid the
pressures and frustrations of our circumstances.

Mindful awareness, per se, is not the ultimate goal or end within Christian practice; rather, we seek a conversion of life that nurtures imaginative engagement and transformation in the fullness of our identity in Christ. Such a converted awareness enables and empowers the experience of a transfigured existence, a reality in which the dimness of our current vision (1 Cor. 13:12) beholds the brightness of Christ's love within us and through us. As the Anglican bishop and theologian Rowan Williams observes, with such a "glimpse" of a transfigured existence, "things become possible."[1] We can face the anxieties and stresses of our lives. We can name the resistances within us that inhibit a greater reliance upon God's grace, becoming less captive to our own ego-driven pursuits and an accomplishment-oriented leadership framework. Above all, we can begin to experience the beauty and truth of the hope that is promised in the consummation of all things, these glimpses of the Spirit of Christ that break through into our existence and that, as Hughes describes, are "still to come as final *pleroma* and commonwealth."[2]

In the moving poem "In a Troubled Time for the Church," the great English Benedictine monk Sebastian Moore paints such a picture of in-breaking hope with images of fire, love, energy, and breath. His words evoke rich images of anticipatory longing, transforming the heart from within:

> To feel the warmth of a consuming fire
> Softens the heart of me to neighbor love
> As the fulfillment of our first desire
> Requiring no commandment from above.
>
> The church's present looking desperate
> Awakes the heart to feel a future God
> And a new sense of what it is to wait
> Dissociating this from the soul's plod.

To wait upon a lover who delays
Is the soul's ecstasy, dark sleepless night
As new energy puzzles and prays
With a new certainty of coming light.

I knew this as there breathed across a psalm
A future against which we do not arm.[3]

The vision of this future fills our eyes and draws our hearts, even as we grapple with current frustrations.

Not "Just" Awareness

One could say that this future orientation indicates a subtle but key distinction between Christian and Buddhist perspectives on mindfulness. As mentioned previously, mindfulness in Buddhist practice is primarily understood as pure, egoless awareness. As Gunaratana says,

> Mindfulness is present-moment awareness. It takes place in the here and now. It is the observance of what is happening right now, in the present. It stays forever in the present, perpetually on the crest of the ongoing wave of passing time.[4]

There are some Buddhist scholars and practitioners who hold there is more to mindfulness practice than *merely* pure awareness. Many Buddhists are aware of the critique that such a self-focused, passive mindfulness practice can be, in reality, self-centered. Diana Winston, the director of mindfulness education at UCLA's Mindful Awareness Research Center and a teacher at Spirit Rock: An Insight Meditation Center, acknowledges some of these possibilities with mindfulness practice, but argues that there are great benefits for continued focus and practice within the Buddhist tradition. As she says,

When we talk about the mindfulness movement, we're not just talking about people paying attention. We're talking about the cultivation of many qualities, which we can think of as "outcome qualities," such as compassion, patience, and equanimity.[5]

It is important to clarify at this point a key argument of this particular book: while in Buddhist practice mindful awareness is primarily understood as pure, egoless awareness *of* reality, within the Christian contemplative tradition, the hope and promise of a transfigured identity is marked by a keen watchfulness *for* the fullness of a reconciled and redeemed existence within Jesus Christ. One should note the difference in orientation within Christianity, as well as the way we are called to participate with the Triune God's dynamic work within our lives. Indeed, this has been a constant refrain at Grace Church as we wrestle with a new way of understanding our vocation. On one hand, we ask ourselves how we can be more *aware of* the challenges and promises of our ministry context while we discern what kind of participation in God's mission we are being *prepared for*. For what embodiment of Christ's love in the world around us is God preparing us? Toward what new possibility of shared ministry are we being equipped, given the pressures and opportunities we face as a community?

Tilden Edwards seeks to illustrate this when he describes the way that our life in Christ broadens our perspective. Using the image of horizons, he states,

> As a Christian, I believe that God's reconciling Spirit in Christ is inviting openness to insights and practices today that expand our horizons in such a way that we find our understanding of Christ, God, and spiritual Reality deepened and widened.[6]

It is the reconciling work of the Spirit of Christ that breathes into our lives and opens our eyes and heart to more of the fullness of what is promised. To be sure, this widening is not a capacity that we have innately within ourselves. In this regard, Robert Hughes's nuanced description of a transfigured awareness and reality is elucidating. For him, understanding spiritual illumination as "transfiguration" is crucial. As he states,

> First, [transfiguration] reminds us that the light of "illumination" is not a "natural" one, neither some natural light of human reason or spirit, nor some inherent light in the created world of nature, but rather the very glory of God illuminating world and self, as they are also illumined from the inside, as it were, by the Holy Spirit indwelling them.[7]

He goes further to clarify that "transfiguration is not transformation, not a magical change of something into what it previously was not but rather the illumination by the light of God's glory of what has always been and remains true."[8] There are, indeed, complex connections here between a Christian understanding of our transfigured identity and a Buddhist understanding of one's Buddha nature. Christianity's theistic interpretation of reality gives rise to a reliance upon God's grace, while Buddhism's nontheistic interpretation of reality emphasizes one's own practice and cultivation of an insightful awareness. Two millennia of Christian theology and spiritual reflection consistently affirms our transfigured identity to be a gift of the Triune God, a grace that draws us into the fullness of God's purpose for our lives.

The reflections offered above by my colleagues articulated just such a sense of God's presence at work in both the search process and the ongoing conversations at Grace. As Cheryl Kelley stated, "I felt the Holy Spirit nudging us along in the whole process, creating a sense of calm under everybody's 'what ifs.'" Cynthia Park testified that "the mindful church model is able to highlight genuine transparency as not only essential to the process but also as an affirmation of the work of the Holy Spirit, focusing human energies toward glorifying God." When Jason Voyles described his experience as senior warden, he noted that we will inevitably face difficult situations in our future. Yet, as he states,

> Rather than have an attitude of gloom and inevitability of some negative occurrence, I see the parish meeting its challenges with enthusiasm and daring to do the hard work of being mindful about where the church's future lies.

Looking back at their separate accounts, it is striking that each of them recognizes the complexities of the current situation and a definite orientation toward future fulfillment. In other words, something is being revealed through increased awareness within our contexts. Even within the more mundane circumstances of vestry meetings and budget preparations, we can catch glimpses of the eschatological reality of Christ shining into our lives.

Exploring the Transfiguration

The Transfiguration story in the Gospel of Matthew reveals this dynamic of a graced awareness unfolding within Peter, James, and John. Jesus takes them "up a high mountain":

> And he was transfigured before them, and his face shone like the sun, and his clothes became a dazzling white. . . . While he was still speaking, suddenly a bright cloud overshadowed them, and from the cloud a voice said, "This is my Son, the Beloved; with him I am well pleased; listen to him!" (Matt. 17:2, 5)

The three disciples realize the profundity of the situation, and they try to grasp and contain it as best they can. Yet they are overcome—overshadowed—by a fullness they cannot imagine.

Rowan Williams describes how, in the Eastern Orthodox tradition, it is common to find the disciples shielding their eyes in iconographic interpretations of this encounter. Their awareness has been heightened, and it is painful. They are beholding what they cannot fully behold. The disciples are faced with the light of Jesus. Williams explains,

> As the Eastern Christian tradition has regularly said, the light that flows from Jesus here is not a 'created' light—it isn't a phenomenon of this world, but a direct encounter with the action of God which alters the whole face of creation precisely because it isn't just another thing in creation. And Peter, James, and John are not ready to see things with and in the light of God, any more than we are.[9]

It is both a disorienting and reorienting heightening of awareness, one that leads us to be "spiritually flung backwards, baffled in finding adequate words for this, even fearful at the prospect of discipleship it puts before us."[10]

As upsetting as such a moment of transfigured awareness might be, it is also an occasion for enormous hope. Again, Williams's words are deeply probing, echoing Tilden Edwards's image of a "door":

> But we are given a glimpse of what God can do in this rare moment of direct vision, when the 'door of perception' is opened by and in Jesus, and the end of the world is fleetingly there before us. And finally, we can let ourselves contemplate the fact that the divine freedom shown us in this vision tells us both that there is not escape from the world in which we have been put as creatures *and* that there is nowhere from which God can be finally exiled.[11]

Such is the nature of awareness seen through the lens of the transfigurative reality of Jesus Christ. It is a posture and practice of illumined alertness and wakefulness—watchfulness—that finds its roots deep within the monastic and contemplative tradition of the Christian faith.

Keep Awake Therefore

Further on in Matthew's gospel account (25:1–13), the story that inspires Sebastian Moore's poetic interpretation of hope in the midst of a "troubled time for the church," we find the evocative account of the ten bridesmaids with lamps and oil, a key text for this recurring meditation on wakefulness and alertness. In this account, we find ten bridesmaids waiting for the arrival of the bridegroom. All have lamps, yet five are described as foolish and five as wise. The five wise bridesmaids have prepared adequately, in a posture of alertness, while the five foolish bridesmaids never prepared for the advent of the bridegroom. When, after hours of waiting, the foolish ones ask for oil to help them fully see and participate in the bridegroom's arrival, they have to leave to go buy oil for themselves, missing the encounter completely. At their return, the door is already closed, and they are left outside the feast. As they cry out to be included in the celebration, Jesus pronounces a summons to a life marked by watchfulness: "Keep awake therefore, for you know neither the day nor the hour" (Matt. 25:13).

Such a posture and practice of watchfulness lies at the heart of the Christian contemplative tradition and is pronounced in patristic texts still highly revered within the broader Orthodox Christian tradition. Within these early texts, one repeatedly encounters the theological concept of *nepsis*, or watchfulness, taken from the Greek root *nepho*, meaning "to keep alert, to stay awake, to remain diligent." George Morelli, a priest within the Antiochian Orthodox Church, articulates *nepsis* in the following terms:

> These early Christian spiritual teachers taught their disciples to develop *nepsis*, that is, to be wakeful and attentive. . . to

that which was inside and around them. Thus, we also need to practice being completely "present" to our own thoughts and surroundings.[12]

As Morelli states, the key component within this practice of prayer or orientation is a "vigilance of the mind and heart." It requires us to become much more aware of our own emotional state and tendency to react in judgment and anger. Elder Ephraim of Philotheou, a contemporary Orthodox theologian at St. Anthony's Greek Orthodox Monastery in Arizona, describes this call to watchfulness in a sermon:

> Abba Paphnoutios, a great father, was going along one day on his way and there he saw two men committing some sin. The thought of his passion said: "Look what great evil they are doing!" The eye saw them and immediately the thought flared up, trying thereby to attack the purity of the Saint's soul by judging the brother or also by his being tempted. Having watchfulness, however, he was being vigilant, immediately his mind was enlightened and he said to his thought, "They are sinning today, I will sin tomorrow. They will repent, but I know myself to be a hard man, unrepentant, egotistical, and thus, I won't repent. I will be punished since I am worse than these two. And what do I have to do about these careless sinners, since I am a much greater sinner and more passionate?" And speaking in this manner and putting a lock on the provocation of sin, he was saved and didn't judge the brothers who were sinning.[13]

Abba Paphnoutios gained a wisdom through his watchfulness, by becoming aware of the temptations at work in the situation rather than by reacting mindlessly to the pressures he faced.

The knowledge or insight Paphnoutios gained is distinctly different from the kind of knowledge we usually gain within our particular circumstances. The knowledge gained by such a *nepsis*-oriented awareness is what the patristic writers deem noetic knowledge. As Morelli explains,

> St. Paul's injunction in his letter to the Romans (12:2), ". . . be transformed by the renewing of your mind. . .," would be understood by an English reader to refer to the rational mind (reason). On the other hand, the Church Fathers would understand that St. Paul is referring to knowledge from the depth of one's heart, which they would call the *nous* or *noetic* mind.[14]

Such a *noetic* transformation springs from openness to the movements of the Holy Spirit in the course of everyday life. Through such a prayerful posture, we can move beyond our ego-driven agendas to gain a wider perspective on whatever circumstances we face. To be sure, for the patristic writers, such a state of awareness was not attained by an innate human faculty operating on its own. As we have already noted, the Christian understanding of illumination differs from Buddhist concepts of mindfulness, even though Buddhist orientations can still yield helpful insights. As Morelli states, "The mindful, noetic, mind of a person is enlightened by an illumination from God, through the Holy Spirit, in the depth of the heart and mind, which allows perception of spiritual experience."[15] Put another way, when our prayer is coupled with a steady practice of *nepsis*, we are led into spaces of transfigured awareness. It is indeed the essence of a transfigured awareness that gives life to one's practice of prayer.

An evocative prayer composed by Archbishop William Temple, now included in the 1979 Book of Common Prayer, seems to ask for just such a comprehensive noetic awareness, embracing heart, mind, imagination, and will.[16] Temple's prayer, moreover, ends with an orientation toward, and availability for, future mission:

> Almighty and eternal God, so draw our hearts to thee, so guide our minds, so fill our imaginations, so control our wills,

that we may be holy thine, utterly dedicated unto thee; and then use us, we pray thee, as thou wilt, and always to thy glory and the welfare of thy people; through our Lord and Savior Jesus Christ. Amen. (BCP, 832–833)

The patristic understanding of *nepsis* would surely nurture conditions in which God's action in drawing in our hearts and granting illumination might fruitfully occur. Further, once our minds are guided, our imaginations are filled, and our wills are controlled, as it were, we then offer ourselves to be used according to the mission of the Triune God who is seeking wholeness for the entire world. One can also see resonances with *nepsis* in the Collect for Purity and the way the cleansing of our heart enables us to magnify God:

Almighty God, to you all hearts are open, all desires known, and from you no secrets are hid: Cleanse the thoughts of our hearts by the inspiration of your Holy Spirit, that we may perfectly love you and worthily magnify your holy Name; through Christ our Lord. Amen. (BCP, 355)

Hope and Health

When we explore the ancient texts of the Christian tradition, we find this eschatologically oriented, attentive posture emphasized by the elders. St. Hesychios of Sinai, now thought to have lived somewhat later than St. John Climacus (sixth or seventh century), wrote a remarkable treatise, "On Watchfulness and Holiness." Commenting on the struggle of the spiritual life, he maintains the necessity of constant reliance upon Christ. As he states,

It is impossible to find the Red Sea among the stars or to walk this earth without breathing air; so too is it impossible to cleanse our heart from impassioned thoughts and to expel its spiritual enemies without the frequent invocation of Jesus Christ.[17]

For Hesychios, purity of heart is the goal of *nepsis*, this state of watchfulness or awareness. In prayer, we come to understand our frailty and our constant struggle with preoccupation and distraction. Our minds focus on the mundane and sinful distractions that surround us in daily life. Without this practice, we persist in a state of spiritual blindness. As he writes,

> Just as a blind man from birth does not see the sun's light, so one who fails to pursue watchfulness does not see the rich radiance of divine grace. He cannot free himself from evil thoughts, words, and actions, and because of these thoughts and actions he will not be able freely to pass the lords of hell when he dies.[18]

Yet we are not without hope, Hesychios says, because the practice of mindfulness is a chosen means by which God comes to our help. "Watchfulness is a spiritual method which . . . completely frees us with God's help from impassioned thoughts, impassioned words, and evil actions."[19] For Hesychios, the practice of *nepsis* undergirds the cultivation of all other virtues: "It is the heart's stillness and, when free from mental images, it is the guarding of the intellect."[20] We are to ground ourselves firmly in Jesus Christ and in the Spirit who gives us life and hope, a grounding that in turn enlivens us and orients us toward the fullness of God rather than the staleness of our more mundane existence.

Nikephoros the Monk, or the Hesychast, who lived in the second half of the thirteenth century, also offers evocative reflections on this essential practice of *nepsis*. He, too, realizes the constant struggle we face in our spiritual practice, the way we too often focus on our own ego-driven preoccupations and succumb to distractions. Yet for Nikephoros as well, hope is ever-present through a practice of watchfulness. For instance, in his treatise "On Watchfulness" he declares,

> For the miracle occurs in tearing ourselves away from the distraction and vain concerns of the world and in this way relentlessly seizing hold of the kingdom of heaven within us.[21]

In a beautiful passage of his work, he shows us that the key to developing such a practice rests in a simple yet close attention to our breath. It is a remarkable visualization exercise:

> You know that what we breathe is air. When we exhale it, it is for the heart's sake, for the heart is the source of life and warmth for the body. The heart draws towards itself the air inhaled when breathing, so that by discharging some of the heat when the air is exhaled it may maintain an even temperature. The cause of this process or, rather, its agent, are the lungs. The Creator has made these capable of expanding and contracting, like bellows, so that they can easily draw in and expel their contents. Thus, by taking in coolness and expelling heat through breathing, the heart performs unobstructed the function for which it was created, that of maintaining life.
>
> Seat yourself, then, concentrate on your intellect, and lead it into the respiratory passage through which your breath passes into your heart. Put pressure on your intellect and compel it to descend with your inhaled breath into your heart. Once it has entered there, what follows will be neither dismal nor glum. Just as a man, after being far away from home, on his return is overjoyed at being with his wife and children again, so the intellect, once it is united with the soul, is filled with indescribable delight.[22]

It is essential to remind ourselves that this transfigured awareness, this *nepsis* of which the patristic writers speak, is not an awareness that is imposed upon the world. It is not an alteration of the world around us into something different; rather, it is the removal of distractions to behold reality as it truly is. It is we who have become blind to the presence of Christ in the world around us. It is this blindness that leads us to rely upon our own ambition and perceived capabilities. Reliance upon ourselves causes stress and anxiety when we face resistances that we mistakenly assume can only be overcome through our own strength. For the ancients, *nepsis*, or transfigured awareness, enables a clearer understanding of the nature of things, freeing us from crippling illusions. As Hesychios teaches, *nepsis* consists of "scrutinizing every mental image," "freeing the heart from all thoughts," "continually and humbly calling upon the Lord Jesus Christ for help," "having the thought of one's death in one's mind," and "fixing one's gaze on heaven."[23]

According to St. Gregory Palamas, the heart of the Transfiguration of Christ consists in realizing the true nature of reality. When St. Gregory discusses the Transfiguration, he explains how it overcomes our blindness:

> Thus Christ was transfigured, not by the addition of something He was not, nor by a transformation into something He was not, but by the manifestation to His disciples of what He really was. He opened their eyes so that instead of being blind they could see. While He himself remained the same, they could now see Him as other than He had appeared to them formerly.[24]

The mystery of the Transfiguration of Christ points to its possibility within our own lives. As we grow through grace in participation in the life of Christ, we are given glimpses of hope that draw us into the fullness of God's promise for the entire world.

A Shifting Perspective on Prayer

There is a temptation in personal prayer to excessive subjectivity, focusing on our desires and preoccupations narrowly conceived. Yet when we lean more into a posture of prayer that is grounded in the *nepsis*-centered, transfigured reality we have described, our orientation shifts. Robert Hughes clarifies the complex interplay between a transparency in prayer that discloses our ordinary human desires and a still deeper desire to align ourselves with God's mission:

> It is not a matter of giving God instructions on how to accomplish our agenda but rather a sharing of our desires and concerns as a means of identifying ourselves with God's agenda, including, I have come to believe, God's own sorrow for the things that do not work out as originally hoped, even as we take new hope and confidence that somehow, "All shall be well."[25]

As Hughes notes, "There is often a shift in prayer in this current of transfiguration."[26] Rather than remaining focused on our own set of requirements, we come to see the deeper connection between God and all of reality. Our perception widens as we come to understand what it means to be part of Christ's Body today as well as what it means for God's reconciling work in Christ to be present throughout the entire world.

The way we understand and yearn for hope takes on new light in the light of Christ. We realize that prayer is not effective because of our efforts or any special skills we imagine we have. Further, prayer does not begin with us but with the Holy Spirit who is already at work in the world, drawing all of existence into the hope of reconciliation and redemption.

More and more we are drawn into a dynamic relationship with the Triune God in our practice of prayer. In a neptic orientation, Hughes explains, our attention shifts "from what is illuminated to the light itself, first contemplating it in its enlightening of others and ourselves but ultimately desiring to know the light in person."[27] In this way, our experience of transfiguration leads to a deepening union with God, to a yearning for a fuller union with the Source of our existence. This "culmination of the spiritual life," as Hughes puts it, "takes on an increasingly erotic dimension, going beyond dalliance to serious courtship."[28]

It is to this dimension that we now turn: a reflection on the practice and understanding of prayer that can cultivate a greater awareness of our union with God and each other within an ordinary or typical parish community that is seeking to reorient the way it understands leadership and ministry. How do we see our desires changing within Grace Church? How do we see our relationships with one another growing through the practice of transfigured awareness? How can we identify the community's yearning for an even deeper grounding in God's presence, given the pressures we face in our day-to-day ministry?

5
Prayer and Desire

This is the basis of hope in moments of despair,
the incentive to carry on when times are out of
joint and men have lost their reason, the source
of confidence when worlds crash and dreams
whiten into ash. The birth of a child—life's most
dramatic answer to death—this is the growing
edge incarnate. Look well to the growing edge!

—**Howard Thurman**, *Meditations of the Heart*

After some four years of conversations and shared ministry, my associate Cynthia and I asked if we could have a conversation with the vestry regarding our own spiritual health. We spoke about how we yearned for a more prayerful conversation around numbers and spiritual health, budgets, and faithfulness. I took the risk of holding up the budget report—as positive as it was—and confessed how I longed for a culture where these numbers did not feel like my annual evaluation. We acknowledged the stress of wanting so badly to see increases in attendance, total membership, and revenue, because these are the default indicators that we, as the clergy and vestry leadership, are somehow "doing a good job." Further, we admitted how we realized the entire Grace community had the luxury of having such a conversation since we were not presently riddled with anxiety about whether or not we would survive much longer as a parish.

Together, we all took the risk of leaning into the conversation and articulating our hopes and dreams of what it would look like, as one vestry member put it, to not to be ruled by the "tyranny of numbers." As I looked around the table, I saw a deep recognition on each face and a shared hope and curiosity about whether such a shift in our communal ethos was even possible. At one point, another vestry member asked the group, "Do we have the power to change the narrative in this way?" In other words, can we set new expectations for our community? Can we hold up new markers for faithfulness, vitality, health, and wholeness? Are we willing to risk stepping into a new territory of measurement? I was so heartened in the conversation, because I saw my colleagues freshly awakening to the possibility of a new way of living and serving together. I felt empowered as we expressed our desire to live and minister with a heightened awareness of the Spirit's guidance of our common life as the Body of Christ. We were aware of the pressures we faced, and we longed to explore the possibility further.

What emerged in that conversation was nothing less than a desire for *theosis*. As the theologian A. M. Allchin reminds us, "Too often we seem to have spoken about God, theorized about him without being able to bring men and women to any living apprehension of his presence and his power."[1] Although the notion of *theosis* is little known within the Anglican tradition, and still less in Protestantism generally, the hope of transforming unity with the Triune God is nonetheless evident in classic Anglican writers and theologians. Theological reflection on *theosis* is of course pronounced within the Orthodox community. Among patristic writers, *theosis* is apprehended as our true and ultimate destiny. All our ascetical work is preparatory for this grace, for it is grace that finally leads us into union with God. As St. Gregory Palamas writes,

> For all the virtue we can attain and such imitation of God
> as lies in our power does no more than fit us for union with

the Deity, but it is through grace that this ineffable union is accomplished.[2]

It was remarkable to glimpse this shared desire emerging from a vestry conversation about deepening our common life of prayer. In my experience, such glimpses within more business-centered meetings are few and far between, and I wondered that night if that absence was due to our negligence in cultivating such a posture of deeper reflection.

It takes enormous risk to engage in such attentive reflection, yet the vista we behold when we pay attention and lean into such transformative encounters is deeply meaningful. Our perspective is indeed widened, and we can catch a glimpse of the profound unity connecting all our lives in Christ. What Allchin described in the writings of key figures in Anglican theology such as Richard Hooker, Lancelot Andrewes, John Wesley, Edward Bouverie Pusey, and John Keble can be seen in our own moments of comparable insight:

> In all we are conscious of a movement of awestruck joy at the presence of God with us and in us, an experience of the dynamic joy of the kingdom which changes all things, overthrowing our customary ways of thinking of the relationships of God with man. From this centre of amazement we gain a new way of looking at things, an alteration of consciousness, a realization that we are able to respond to the world's problems when we see that in the power of the gospel the problems themselves are being changed and that we ourselves are in the process of changing.[3]

Our shared vision is enhanced as our spiritual myopia is addressed and repaired. Together, we are challenged to trust even more the Spirit's guidance, as we catch a glimpse of what God can make possible. Eventually, through this grace, we come to see that our yearning for God is fueled, in reality, by God's yearning for us!

It is this dynamic of yearning that is the beating heart of our work within the parish community. All our hope for a more imaginative experience rooted in discernment, for a mindful engagement with our vocation, and for the promised hope of a transfigured awareness within Christ enables us to comprehend more fully our deepest desire: union with God.

Our conversations were deeply important for us, and we realized the absolute necessity of grounding these conversations in a practice of common prayer. We named out loud that the only way we could truly explore our desire for a sharpened awareness of our unity in Christ was to take crucial steps as leaders of the parish.

We reflected together that our practice of watchfulness can only be supported by a posture of constant prayer. Only by such faithful practice can we hope to become more aware of the circumstances of our lives, resist the pressure to capitulate to a success-oriented pro-gram emphasis, and respond to the opportunity for a conversion to another way of living in the Spirit of Christ. Our longing for a life resonant with God's dream is rooted in God's own being. As Allchin writes, "He longs for his people, delights to dwell among them, finds in them his joy."[4] Together we began to realize that the practice of *nepsis*, of watchfulness that leads to transfigured life in Christ, enables us to lay hold of our deepest desire. Put another way, when my vestry colleague asked if we had the power to change the narrative, this very question was rooted in her desire for a shared ministry springing from an awareness of our union with God in Christ.

What Do You Desire Most?

From such a place of vulnerability, we were able to ask ourselves a critical question: "What do we desire most?" We looked back over our previous conversations and found a subtle thread connecting much of our common work. Underneath the question asked in the listening circles—"What have been the most meaningful experiences in your life with _____?"—lay a still deeper invitation to reflect on our desires to see our children, youth, and adults come to a greater awareness of Christ's presence in their lives. Underneath the search committee's work lay the same deep engagement about what they and the parish desired, not just with a new rector but for the entire community.

Finally, in these times of institutional challenge and sociopolitical pressure, we are also invited to reflect more deeply on the nature of our heart's desire. Desire, we come to see, lies at the heart of all we do: our desire for greater union with God and his purposes for our lives as well as our bourgeoning awareness of God's profound desire for us—to bring our entire lives into the fullness of God's very being.

According to Allchin, this desire for union with God reorients our entire vision and understanding of reality:

> The Christian tradition is thus full of an affirmation of God's nearness to humankind, and of our unrealized potential for God. The basic affirmations that Jesus is Lord, Jesus is the Christ, are affirmations about the possibilities of man, about the intimacy of relationship between human and divine, no less than about the mystery of God. They speak about a meeting, a union of God with humankind that alters our understanding, our deepest experience of what it is to be human, which gives us a new vision of the whole creation and alters the substance of our living and dying.[5]

Union with God is at the heart of our deepest desire, yet our lives more often than not fall far short of this reality because of human frailty, blindness, and sin. The English Benedictine monk Sebastian Moore speaks eloquently about this dynamic of desire and those things that work against it:

> God is a god of desire, not of power and prestige, and Jesus
> knew God as the object of all our deepest desires—for joy, for
> laughter, and the love of friends, for sexual fulfillment. All of
> his life and teaching can be summarized as encouraging us to
> allow our innate desire, which is also God's desire for us, to
> break through our fear and self-loathing. And sin is that fear,
> fear of desire, fear of life and fear of falling into God.[6]

Moore argues that "we are wired for love and we only flourish
when we love."[7] Desire is the fundamental characteristic of our identity as human beings, this yearning within us for complete fulfillment. The tension within our lives comes from straying from our
heart's desire and instead settling for the distractions of the surround-
ing world. This desire pulses between us and God, and we can feel it
deep within us.

Jesus, Moore argues, lived in absolute attunement with this deepest yearning within the human heart. He knew the fullness of human
potential as well as the propensity to fall far short of God's dream for
us all. Jesus, Moore writes,

> dreamed of a society ruled by desire as he knew it, and not
> by the myriad forces that come to rule the world forgetful of
> real desire and forever sinking into its counterfeits. What we
> call sin is the enormous darkness everywhere, the worldwide
> conspiracy to turn our back on what we most deeply know
> about ourselves.[8]

As much as Jesus recognized our potential, Jesus also knew of the
terrible possibility of our missing the mark. He was vividly aware of
the persistent push and pull within humanity, an awareness perhaps
nowhere better embodied than at his very crucifixion between two
thieves, each embodying this tension themselves in their last moments
of life.

The Eucharistic Heart of Our Common Life

The significance of entering into such an intimate indwelling in God's very self is far too often missed within the minutiae of parish ministry, yet the promised hope of our participation in the eschatological banquet is the essence of the Eucharist. Our experience of the Eucharist is greatly enriched by the practice of watchfulness, as St. Hesychios teaches it. In accord with an imaginative engagement that nurtures a transfiguration of our awareness, St. Hesychios envisions the "divine fire, the body of our Lord Jesus Christ," driving away the illusions of our lives. Such illusions capture our attention, drawing our attention away from our true desires and leaving us, ultimately, unfulfilled. Through attention to the promised presence of Christ in the Eucharist, we become attuned to fullness of life in Christ himself.

> And if after this, standing at the entrance to our heart, we keep strict watch over the intellect, when we are again permitted to receive those Mysteries the divine body will illumine our intellect still more and make it shine like a star.[9]

Such a development in ourselves, guided by the Holy Spirit, enables a fuller participation—a significant appreciation—of the eucharistic heart of our faith. We become aware of distractions, hesitancies, and preoccupations that thwart such an experience of sacramental significance—our deeper desire. As Julia Gatta, a professor of pastoral theology at the School of Theology, points out, the distraction we experience during our preparation for the Eucharist mirrors the inattention we experience within wider life, noting "the atmosphere in sacristies prior to the eucharist, where too often pandemonium reigns."[10] What priest has not experienced the cacophony of voices, urgent demands for appointments, questions about upcoming Sunday classes, and frustrated opinions on recent decisions hurled their way as they drape the chasuble over themselves and prepare to process into the nave? But it does not have to be this way.

Even though we suffer from the onslaught of anxiety within the wider culture, we have the opportunity within our parish communities to reorient ourselves in our liturgy with intentional periods of silence. It is helpful, for instance, to hold significant pauses before praying the collects, before the confession, after the sermon, and after the reception of Holy Communion, which can be experienced as a moment of communal mystical, sacramental union with Christ. A parish that incorporates a few simple, corporately agreed-upon disciplines, such as intentional boundary-keeping in the vesting space itself and maintaining a prayerful silence before the liturgy begins, will find their experience of the liturgy immeasurably deepened. "Pacing the liturgy to the measure of the Spirit is fundamental," Gatta writes.[11] The same can be said of our entire framework of administration and ministry: pauses before meetings, silence before vestry decisions, and dedicated times of study and shared prayer can guide the tone of an administrative staff. In this way, our approach to the eucharistic celebration gives shape to the entire spectrum of the parish's common life. Gatta's hopeful image is enticing:

> The task here is to embody, through posture and demeanor, such calm and focused attention that we absorb the Word of God ourselves and invite others to do the same. As we listen or pray, we become conscious of Christ's presence—among us, surrounding us, within us.[12]

Such focused attention to Christ's presence across the various movements of the liturgy teaches a way of praying that congregants can then carry over into personal prayer. For as the twentieth-century Christian mystic Evelyn Underhill observes, "The spirit of prayer is far more easily caught than taught."[13]

Gatta's use of the word *absorb* is interesting, because it points to the way our lives instead soak up the flavor of the world around us. Why should we be surprised that many churches rely on corporate leadership models when that is the dominant secular paradigm? Why should we be surprised when parish clergy and vestry members become fixated on numeric indicators to gauge the health and vitality of a spiritual community when such expectations pervade our collective consciousness? Yet as a community sacramentally nourished by the presence of Jesus Christ in the Eucharist, we are constantly invited to reimagine our assumptions about ourselves and our ministries.

Sebastian Moore poses a question for us in the church and in the world as we reflect on the goodness of Jesus within our lives: "Can we experience our desire to love all people that Jesus brings to flourishing in the *ecclesia* of the called?"[14] Can we notice this yearning within us and then seek to embody it around us and within us, with all whom we meet? Can we nurture this deeper yearning and thus reorient the way we understand discipleship and ministry? It is a question of discernment, watchfulness, and vocation.

> With Jesus revealing us to ourselves as seated where he is in the heavenly places, we have a new definition of sin, not as the breaking of a law but as the *frustrating of our real desire* (Moore's emphasis).[15]

A Practice of "Focusing"

In a meaningful connection to our prior discussion on mindfulness and *nepsis*, or watchfulness, within the patristic tradition, Moore describes an intriguing practice called "focusing" that he uses to engage this tension directly. In situations where we find ourselves aware of a struggle, when we become aware of both a potential for growth as well as any fear, anger, or resistance that is present, we are invited to lean into the experience with our bodies, our own embodied existence. What is going on inside us? What are we feeling toward the situation, toward others around us? As we become more aware of what we feel in the situation, we remind ourselves of Jesus's words. As Moore says, "'Do not be afraid!' and 'Open now to one another!' are the same command to live in our new condition of human flourishing, for which Christ is the pioneer, as the Letter to the Hebrews says."[16]

We are invited to be honest with ourselves, trusting that the pain of our own circumstance finds its hope and restoration within the reality of Jesus, who yearns to draw us into the dynamic life of the Triune God. In this space of honest awareness, we see what is possible.

> The point of focusing is that this "me" thus attended to, thus listened to, what [Eckhart] Tolle calls my "pain-body," is where desire resides and wants to grow into loving. OK, so I go there and let this happen.[17]

Much honesty and vulnerability is demanded of us to enter into such a space of restoration and union. We need not deny our pain, anger, grief, and frustration—indeed we cannot—in order to yield to God's invitation to be united through Christ into the fullness intended for us. Such an image of our entire selves being enveloped in the mystery of Christ's own birth, life, death, and resurrection harken to Paul's Letter to the Philippians when he imagines the potential of being united with Christ in the Paschal Mystery that gives all our faith shape and sustenance:

> I want to know Christ and the power of his resurrection and the sharing of his sufferings by becoming like him in his death, if somehow I may attain the resurrection from the dead. Not that I have already obtained this or have already

reached the goal; but I press on to make it my own, because
Christ Jesus has made me his own. Beloved, I do not consider that I have made it my own; but this one thing I do:
forgetting what lies behind and straining forward to what
lies ahead, I press on towards the goal for the prize of the
heavenly call of God in Christ Jesus. (Phil. 3:10–14)

To return to the beginning of this reflection, we need not deny the
frustrations and fears that arise when we face the circumstances and
pressures of church attendance and budgetary challenges—nor the
loss of any perceived cultural sway. Rather than denying these points
of stress, Moore would encourage us to be curious about what lay just
on the other side of them: our deeper yearning. Such a space of honesty is the place of the cross and the tomb, the space that gives rise to
new life and promise. By engaging our deepest yearning, our desire to
become our real and full selves within God, we can place the reality
of our lives before the reality of Christ himself. In that moment of
awareness, when the stone of the tomb rolls away, the hope for a new
way of being is realized. As Moore illustrates,

There is an unmistakable shock, of disorientation, of terror;
something new and unmanageable is breaking in. And who
is this figure that people don't recognize until something
happens inside them? Sound familiar? You don't know him
till the real you wakes up, and then he vanishes, leaving you
with the breaking of bread, the light in the eyes, the heart
on fire, the Kingdom, the world the way it is meant to be.
And then the shock of the empty tomb reveals its secret.
It is the shock of recovering from a sickness as old as the
world, the new breaking-in on the oldest thing we know,
the place of the dead, emptying the tomb and the mind
to receive him, the man of our desire, the true shape of
the world.[18]

Moore says that we should pray that "the real you wakes up." Then we can step into the new reality promised by and embodied in the risen Christ.

It may not be readily evident that the conversations, hopes, struggles, and dreams of an ordinary group of church people find their deepest meaning within such an understanding of desire. "Why not?" I would ask. Why do we not see the potential of typical, normal, routine parish ministry as the grounds for such a dynamic of discernment, mindfulness, watchfulness, transfiguration, and union? What is the point of our shared life together if not for "all of us [to] come to the unity of the faith and of the knowledge of the Son of God, to maturity, to the measure of the full stature of Christ" (Eph. 4:13)?

Sadly, church communities often fall victim to the same cycle of program maintenance and anxiety-driven predictability as any secular enterprise.[19] Our days become filled with the common stresses around attendance, budget demands, and building maintenance. In a world where our norm is now articulated as "decline," this becomes an inevitable focus. Yet the call of Christ persists, the invitation to a fuller participation in the very life of God who seeks our wholeness and vitality. We are given the opportunity to have our eyes opened to see the potential for conversion within the minutiae of mundane ministry. We need not deny the pain and frustration we feel; rather, we can lean into our reality and trust that the Spirit of Christ is already at work, bringing to life that which we thought was hopeless.

Such is our hope, the promise we are given by God in Christ, and it is very much an meaningful way to share in parish ministry! It is the promise of our sacramental life—drenched in the waters of Baptism and nourished with the bread and wine of the Eucharist—that invigorates us and guides us into the fullness God dreams for us as individuals and as a community of faith.

EPILOGUE
Vocation and Emptying

*I will utter Your name, sitting alone among the
shadows of my thoughts. I will utter it without
words; I will utter it without purpose. For I am like
a child that calls its mother a hundred times, glad
that it can say, "Mother."*

—**Rabindranath Tagore**, *The Heart of God*

The central question of this book has been to wonder together how
we can understand our vocation as both clergy and laity in the church
today. How can the church understand our collective vocation in the
midst of the particular challenges we face as a society? What language
can we explore? What practices? What risks can we take to embark on
a new, fresh way of understanding our prayer and embodiment in this
world? What are we called to be aware of, and how does this awareness
empower us to live transfigured lives that are grounded in hope? What
are we being called to nurture, and what are we being called to release?

In theological language, "having a vocation" means recognizing
that God is calling each of us into a life of particular service, grounded
in our common realization of our union with God and one another
in Christ Jesus. This union reorients us to see all life as interconnected, even as so many forces around us seem driven to separate and
diminish. We all have a vocation, even if clergy are more public about
theirs—for better or worse.

The heart of my vocation lies in this recognition of God's indwelling presence, a reality that frames the way I understand my own struggles and desires, my tendencies for grasping and my yearning to relax in the graciousness of God's embrace. I will stumble and fall in any embodiment of ministry if I am not grounded in the Spirit's call: the trustworthy movement of the Living Spirit of Christ that infuses all of life and calls me to share in it. Perhaps it is even more honest to say I will stumble and fall *more painfully* if I am not grounded as such, since stumbling and falling is a given with my sinfulness I know all too well.

Perhaps herein lies the ultimate struggle for those of us in the institutional or traditional church at this point in our lives: Can we trust in the Spirit's movement and practice a certain yielding to the movement of divine grace? While I cannot find "yielding" or "consenting" on any list of necessary skills for effective ministers, I think it is an essential practice to consider. When it comes to "being church," only when we yield our urge to grasp what has been can we make room in our hearts for where the Spirit is leading us. Only when we consent to the Spirit's guidance can we prayerfully guard against our own willful ignorance and arrogance.

As a very educated white man, in particular, what am I being called to yield as I recognize the needed awareness and transformation in our broader society today? What healing can I nurture even as I discern the way that oppressive and constrictive structures are broken down to make way for the Spirit to move more freely? How can my contemplative practice anchor me in the compassion of Christ even in moments when my ego is pinched and I feel myself grasping for old patterns of what Fr. Thomas Keating described so often as our "emotional programs for happiness"? These egoic postures seek to reaffirm our patterns of seeking safety and security, affirmation and esteem, and power and control.

The practicing of yielding and consenting on an institutional level reminds me of a conversation we shared with Fr. Thomas Keating as part of the New Contemplative Exchange at St. Benedict's Monastery in Snowmass, Colorado, in August 2017. On one particular day, five of us went to see Fr. Thomas in the periodical room at the monastery. He was tired, but he spent over an hour with us and listened deeply to what each of us was wondering in our respective contexts. He felt empowered to share with us his hope for how the wisdom of the contemplative tradition—the heart of a radical trust in the Spirit's invitation to a deeper awareness of the unitive vision of reality—might speak to the challenges we were facing in the world today.

He shared with us that we were called to participate in the very life of God, to partake in God's own life within the realities of our own. The intimacy we experience with God, that we see in the mutual indwelling of the Trinity, invites us to a certain point where, as he said, there is an awareness that there is no division between you and God. There is not, he said, numerically one; rather, the intimacy between us is a sharing in the richness of the Divine Indwelling.

As we sat there, I couldn't resist suddenly saying, "Well, that's a lot to live up to!" He laughed and told me, "That's the thing. You don't have to live up to anything, because the secret of Christian life is to lose yourself. To lose yourself in God."

Those who lose their life will find it, Jesus teaches. The path of self-emptying is the path that leads to this awareness of our union with God and one another. Fr. Thomas went on to say that we are not only called to lose just one part of our lives but our whole selves, our whole embodied being that is plagued by our grasping tendencies. We cannot grasp, because then we truly do lose hold of the deeper truth of our existence: that we are all being held together in God's loving embrace.

So, in the end, I am left with more questions: What are we being called to let go of as a parish church and Christian community so that we can be filled even more with the fullness of God's love?

What emptying are we being invited into with regards to our structures and customs, that will nurture such a radical awareness of God's love for us, a love that truly will reform the way we understand ministry for the coming age? How are we called to trust the Spirit?

Notes

1 Context and the Challenge

1. Bhante Gunaratana, *Mindfulness in Plain English* (Boston: Wisdom Publications, 2011), 134–35. There are myriad resources on mindfulness and meditation practices, and I won't list all the sources I have found meaningful in this book. There are many lineages and traditions within Buddhism that all contain enormous wisdom and insight into the cultivation of awareness and compassion. In particular, I commend to you the work of the Mind and Life Institute and their ongoing work and resources that are both scholarly and practice-oriented.

2. Gunaratana, *Mindfulness in Plain English*, 135.

3. Gunaratana, 135

4. Gunaratana, 134–35.

5. Sebastian Moore, "Some Principles for an Adequate Theism," *Downside Review* 95, no. 320 (July 1977): 206. Rowan Williams references Moore in his reflection on how the core of the Christian faith lies with the complex relationship of desire rather than in a more severe notion of "God's will." See Rowan Williams, *The Wound of Knowledge* (London: Darton, Longman and Todd, 1990), 130. Moore's image of God's "wanting-to-be" in our lives underscores God's desire for us, and our reciprocal desire for God and participation in God's mission and purpose within our lives. This image of desire is a crucial one that will become central in later chapters of this work.

2 Discernment and Imagination

1. There has been much research over the past decade that is helpful. See research from the Pew Research Center for a thorough analysis of the situation around declining church participation. Specifically, the article "'Nones' on the Rise," October 9, 2012, http://www.pewforum.org /2012/10/09/nones-on-the-rise/. Later surveys only reinforce the

trends we have been witnessing. See also Luis Lugo, "The Decline of Institutional Religion" (presentation, Faith Angle Forum, South Beach, FL, March 18, 2013); https://www.washingtonpost.com/r/2010-2019 /WashingtonPost/2013/03/25/Editorial-Opinion/Graphics /Pew-Decline-of-Institutional-Religion.pdf. and Pew Research Center, "America's Changing Religious Landscape," Pew Research Center (website), May 12, 2015, http://www.pewforum.org/2015/05/12 /americas-changing-religious-landscape/. The Pew Research Center delves deeply into the data, showing the complexity of the phenomenon within the United States as well as the broader Western world. You may also explore recent surveys completed by the Fetzer Institute that show the remarkable complexity of how diverse Americans view the importance of "spirituality": Veronica Selzler, *What Does Spirituality Mean to Us?* (Kalamazoo, MI: Fetzer Institute, 2020), https:// spiritualitystudy.fetzer.org/.

2. Abraham Joshua Heschel, *God in Search of Man: A Philosophy of Judaism* (New York: Farrar, Straus and Giroux, 1976), 3. See also, Terri A. Valing in the foreword to *Way to Water: A Theopoetics Primer*, by L. Callid Keefe-Perry (Eugene, OR: Cascade Books, 2014), xvi.

3. Ronald Heifetz et al., *The Practice of Adaptive Leadership: Tools and Tactics for Changing Your Organization and the World* (Boston: Harvard Business Press, 2009), 71–73, 307. I find this particular work useful in its differentiation of "technical" and "adaptive" techniques of leadership development, but I argue the need for a fuller recovery and practice of the contemplative and transformational aspects of leadership and practice within the broader Christian tradition.

4. Amos Wilder, *Theopoetic: Theology and Religious Imagination* (Lima, OH: Academic Renewal Press, 2001), 6.

5. Wilder, 6–7.

6. L. Callid Keefe-Perry, *Way to Water: A Theopoetics Primer* (Eugene, OR: Cascade Books, 2014), 6.

7. Tilden Edwards, *Valuing and Nurturing a Mind-in-Heart Way: The Promise of a Contemplatively-Oriented Seminary* (Washington, DC: Shalem Institute, 2010), 1.

8. Edwards, *Valuing and Nurturing a Mind-in-Heart Way*, 1.

9. Edwards, 4.

10. Edwards, 4.

11. Thomas C. Oden, *Pastoral Theology: Essentials of Ministry* (San Francisco: HarperCollins, 1983), 4.

12. Oden, *Pastoral Theology*, 153.

13. Edwards, *Valuing and Nurturing a Mind-in-Heart Way*, 7.

14. Edwards, 40.

15. Edwards, 5.

16. George J. Schemel and Judith A. Roemer, "Communal Discernment," *Review for Religious* 40, no 6 (July 1992): 6.

17. Schemel and Roemer, "Communal Discernment," 12.

18. Schemel and Roemer, 7.

19. Schemel and Roemer, 16.

20. Tilden Edwards, *Embracing the Call to Spiritual Depth: Gifts for Contemplative Living* (New York: Paulist Press, 2010), 49.

21. Edwards, *Embracing the Call to Spiritual Depth*, 124.

3 Mindfulness and Conversion

1. Jeff Wilson, *Mindful America: The Mutual Transformation of Buddhist Meditation and American Culture* (New York: Oxford University Press, 2014), 39.

2. Wilson, *Mindful America*, 77.

3. Wilson, 11.

4. Bhante Gunaratana, *Mindfulness in Plain English* (Boston: Wisdom Publications, 2011), 42.

5. See also the many works of S. N. Goenka, one of the world's foremost teachers of vipassana meditation.

6. Gunaratana, *Mindfulness in Plain English*, 26.

7. Gunaratana, 26.

8. Gunaratana, 27.

9. Gunaratana, 23.

10. Gunaratana, 24.

11. Gunaratana, 25.

12. Tilden Edwards, *Embracing the Call to Spiritual Depth: Gifts for Contemplative Living* (New York: Paulist Press, 2010), 6.

13. Edwards, *Embracing the Call to Spiritual Depth*, 7.

14. Edwards, 6.

15. Edwards, 6–7.

16. Edwards, 6.

17. Amos Wilder, *Theopoetic: Theology and Religious Imagination* (Lima, OH: Academic Renewal Press, 2001), 7.

18. The work of the Society for the Increase of the Ministry is important work in the Episcopal Church and beyond, as it explores ways to support and enrich the formation of leaders in a widening setting of church leadership.

19. Edwards, *Embracing the Call to Spiritual Depth*, 73.

20. Edwards, 73.

21. Robert Davis Hughes, *Beloved Dust: Tides of the Spirit in the Christian Life* (New York: Continuum, 2008), 92.

22. Walter Brueggemann was my Old Testament professor at Columbia Theological Seminary. He used this phrase to describe the condition of the society against which the prophetic tradition spoke. For any change in the socio-religious establishment to occur, such a state of psychic numbness must first be identified and then engaged.

23. Hughes, *Beloved Dust*, 77.

24. Hughes, 78.

25. Hughes, 71.

4 Transfiguration and Illumination

1. Rowan Williams, "The Transfiguration," in *The Dwelling of the Light: Praying with Icons of Christ* (Grand Rapids, MI: Williams B. Eerdmans, 2003), 9–10.

2. Robert Davis Hughes, *Beloved Dust: Tides of the Spirit in the Christian Life* (New York: Continuum, 2008), 385.

3. Sebastian Moore, *The Contagion of Christ: Doing Theology as If It Mattered* (Maryknoll, NY: Orbis Books, 2007), 184.

4. Bhante Gunaratana, *Mindfulness in Plain English* (Boston: Wisdom Publications, 2011), 134.

5. Diana Winston, "Forum: What Does Mindfulness Mean for Buddhism?" *Lion's Roar*, May 5, 2015, http://www.lionsroar.com/forum-what-does-mindfulness-mean-for-buddhism/. Indeed, one thinks of Thich Nhat Hanh's work with "engaged Buddhism" as well and the intersection of meditation practice and social compassion found in other recent embodiments of Buddhism.

6. Tilden Edwards, *Embracing the Call to Spiritual Depth: Gifts for Contemplative Living* (New York: Paulist Press, 2010), 19.

7. Hughes, *Beloved Dust*, 257.

8. Hughes, 258.

9. Williams, *Dwelling of the Light*, 13. See also Solrunn Nes, *The Uncreated Light: An Iconographical Study of the Transfiguration in the Eastern Church* (Grand Rapids, MI: Eerdmans, 2007). Nes reflects on the artistic and imaginative aspects of pivotal iconography within the broader tradition, drawing on rich theological reflections to aid in the development of a practice of prayer.

10. Williams, *Dwelling of the Light*, 16.

11. Williams, 18.

12. George Morelli, "Mindfulness as Known by the Church Fathers," Antiochian Orthodox Christian Archdiocese of North America, accessed October 11, 2016, http://ww1.antiochian.org/mindfulness-known-church-fathers.

13. Ephraim of Philotheou, "Watchfulness, Prayer, and Confession," trans. Seraphim Bell, Orthodox Christian Information Center, accessed October 11, 2016, http://www.orthodoxinfo.com/praxis/elderephraimhomily1.aspx.

14. Morelli, "Mindfulness."

15. Morelli, "Mindfulness."

16. Marion J. Hatchett, *Commentary on the American Prayer Book* (1980; repr., San Francisco: HarperSanFrancisco, 1995), 568.

17. Hesychios the Priest, "On Watchfulness and Holiness," in *The Philokalia: The Complete Texts*, vol. 1, trans. and ed. G. E. H. Palmer, Philip Sherrard, and Kallistos Ware (New York: Farrar, Straus, and Giroux, 1979), 166.

18. Hesychios the Priest, "On Watchfulness and Holiness," 163.

19. Hesychios the Priest, 162.

20. Hesychios the Priest, 162–63.

21. Nikephoros, "On Watchfulness," *Philokalia*, vol. 1, 194.

22. Nikephoros, 205.

23. Hesychios, "On Watchfulness and Holiness," 164–65.

24. Gregory of Palamas, "The Declaration of the Holy Mountain," *Philokalia*, vol. 4, 422.

25. Hughes, *Beloved Dust*, 338.

26. Hughes, 338.

27. Hughes, 338. I also find Richard Rohr's recent book *The Universal Christ: How a Forgotten Reality Can Change Everything We See, Hope For, and Believe* very meaningful in its description of this Light of Christ that illuminates all of existence.

28. Hughes, *Beloved Dust*, 339.

5 Prayer and Desire

1. A. M. Allchin, *Participation in God: A Forgotten Strand in Anglican Tradition* (London: Darton, Longman and Todd, 1988), 1.

2. Gregory Palamas, "The Declaration of the Holy Mountain in Defence of Those Who Devoutly Practise a Life of Stillness," *Philokalia*, vol. 4, 421.

3. Allchin, *Participation in God*, 4.

4. Allchin, *Participation in God*, 65.

5. Allchin, 63.

6. Sebastian Moore, *The Contagion of Christ: Doing Theology as If It Mattered* (Maryknoll, NY: Orbis Books, 2007), 120.

7. Moore, *Contagion of Christ*, 120.

8. Moore, 121.

9. Hesychios, "On Watchfulness and Holiness," *Philokalia*, vol. 1, 179.

10. Julia Gatta, *The Nearness of God: Parish Ministry as Spiritual Practice* (New York: Morehouse Publishing, 2010), 52.

11. Gatta, *Nearness of God*, 42. See also the many works of Martin Smith and his insightful reflections on pastoral ministry and the practice of prayer. Gatta and Smith are invaluable resources for congregational ministry.

12. Gatta, 42.

13. Evelyn Underhill, "The Parish Priest and the Life of Prayer," reprinted in *The Mount of Purification* (London: Longmans, Green, 1960), 265–67; cited in Gatta, *Nearness of God*, 52. Howard Thurman once made a similar statement in an interview on the dynamics of spiritual practice.

14. Moore, *Contagion of Christ*, 115.

15. Moore, 114.

16. Moore, 115. The American philosopher and psychologist Eugene Gendlin pioneered this practice of focusing, and I commend his work to you.

17. Moore, 118.

18. Moore, 123–24.

19. I commend to you the recent work done by Bobbi Patterson, an Episcopal priest and retired professor at Emory University: *Building Resilience through Contemplative Practice: A Field Manual for Helping Professionals and Volunteers* (New York: Routledge, 2020). Patterson's work is insightful in the way it connects contemplative practice, from both the Christian and Buddhist traditions, with case studies that challenge our typical patterns of success and accomplishment within ministry.

Suggestions for Further Reading

Allchin, A. M. *The Joy of All Creation*. Cambridge, MA: Cowley, 1984.

———. *Participation in God: A Forgotten Strand in Anglican Tradition*. London: Darton, Longman & Todd, 1988.

———. *The World Is a Wedding: Explorations in Christian Spirituality*. New York: Oxford University Press, 1978.

Augustine of Hippo. *On Free Choice of the Will*. Translated by Thomas Williams. Indianapolis, IN: Hackett, 1993.

Bahnson, Fred. *Soil and Sacrament: A Spiritual Memoir of Food and Faith*. New York: Simon & Schuster, 2013.

Brown, Lerita Coleman. *When the Heart Speaks, Listen: Discovering Inner Wisdom*. Castroville, TX: Black Rose Writing, 2019.

Bucko, Adam, ed. *Holy Thirst: Essentials of Carmelite Spirituality*. Brewster, MA: Paraclete Press, 2019.

Coakley, Sarah. *God, Sexuality, and the Self: An Essay "On the Trinity."* Cambridge, UK: Cambridge University Press, 2013.

Collins, Billy. "Introduction to Poetry." In *The Apple That Astonished Paris*. Fayetteville: University of Arkansas Press, 1996.

Edwards, Tilden. *Embracing the Call to Spiritual Depth: Gifts for Contemplative Living*. New York: Paulist Press, 2010.

———. *Valuing and Nurturing a Mind-in-Heart Way: The Promise of a Contemplatively-Oriented Seminary*. Washington, DC: Shalem Institute, 2010.

Ephraim of Philotheou. "Watchfulness, Prayer, and Confession." Translated by Seraphim Bell. http://www.orthodoxinfo.com/praxis/elderephraimhomily1.aspx.

Francis, Pope. *Laudato si': On Care for Our Common Home.* Washington, DC: United States Conference of Catholic Bishops, 2015.

Gatta, Julia. *The Nearness of God: Parish Ministry as Spiritual Practice.* New York: Morehouse Publishing, 2010.

Gunaratana, Bhante. *Mindfulness in Plain English.* Boston, MA: Wisdom Publications, 2011.

Hanh, Thich Nhat. *The Miracle of Mindfulness: A Manual on Meditation.* Boston, MA: Beacon Press, 1987.

Hatchett, Marion J. *Commentary on the American Prayer Book.* New York: Seabury Press, 1980. Reprint, San Francisco: HarperSanFrancisco, 1995.

Heifetz, Ronald et al. *The Practice of Adaptive Leadership: Tools and Tactics for Changing Your Organization and the World.* Boston, MA: Harvard Business School, 2009.

Herbert, George. "Love Bade Me Welcome." In *The Country Parson/The Temple.* Edited by John N. Wall, Jr. New York: Paulist Press, 1981.

Holmes, Urban T. III, *Ministry and Imagination.* New York: Seabury Press, 1981.

Hughes, Robert Davis III. *Beloved Dust: Tides of the Spirit in the Christian Life.* New York: Continuum, 2008.

Keefe-Perry, L. Callid. *Way to Water: A Theopoetics Primer.* Eugene, OR: Cascade Books, 2014.

Leech, Kenneth. *True Prayer: An Invitation to Christian Spirituality.* London: Sheldon Press, 1980. Reprint, New York: Morehouse Publishing, 1995.

Lugo, Luis. "The Decline of Institutional Religion." Pew Research Forum. March 18, 2013. http://www.eppc.s3.amazonaws.com/wp-content/uploads/2013/07/LugoPresentation.pdf.

McColman, Carl. *The Big Book of Christian Mysticism: The Essential Guide to Contemplative Spirituality.* Charlottesville, VA: Hampton Roads, 2010.

Mingyur, Yongey, and Helen Tworkov. *In Love with the World: A Monk's Journey Through the Bardos of Living and Dying.* New York: Speigel and Grau, 2019.

Moore, Sebastian. *The Contagion of Christ: Doing Theology As If It Mattered.* Maryknoll, NY: Orbis Books, 2007.

———. "Some Principles for an Adequate Theism." *The Downside Review* 95 (July 1977): 201–13.

Morelli, George. "Mindfulness as Known by the Church Fathers." Antiochian Orthodox Christian Archdiocese. http://www.antiochian.org/mindfulness-known-church-fathers.

Nes, Solrunn. *The Uncreated Light: An Iconographical Study of the Transfiguration in the Eastern Church.* Grand Rapids, MI: William B. Eerdmans, 2007.

Oden, Thomas. *Pastoral Theology: Essentials of Ministry.* San Francisco: HarperCollins, 1983.

Palmer, G. E. H., and Philip Sherrard, and Kallistos Ware, ed. and trans. *The Philokalia: The Complete Texts.* 4 vols. New York: Farrar, Straus, and Giroux, 1979.

Panikkar, Raimon. *Christophany: The Fullness of Man.* Maryknoll, NY: Orbis Books, 2010.

———. *The Experience of God: Icons of the Mystery.* Minneapolis: Fortress Press, 2006.

Patterson, Bobbi. *Building Resilience Through Contemplative Practice: A Field Manual for Helping Professionals and Volunteers.* New York: Routledge, 2020

Pew Research Forum. "America's Changing Religious Landscape." Pew Research Center. May 12, 2015. http://wwwpewforum.org/2015/05/12/americas-changing-religious-landscape/.

———. "Nones on the Rise." Pew Research Center. October 9, 2012. http://www.pewforum.org/2012/10/09/nones-on-the-rise/.

Rilke, Rainer Maria. *Rilke's Book of Hour: Love Poems to God.* Translated by Anita Barrows and Joanna Macy. New York: Riverhead Books, 2005.

Rohr, Richard. *The Universal Christ: How a Forgotten Reality Can Change Everything We See, Hope For, and Believe.* New York: Convergent Books, 2019.

Schemel, George J., and Judith A. Roemer. "Communal Discernment." *Review for Religious* 40, no. 6, (1992): 1–23.

Smith, Jessie, and Stuart Higginbotham. *Contemplation and Community: A Gathering of Fresh Voices for a Living Tradition.* New York: Crossroad, 2019.

Smith, Martin L. *The Word Is Very Near You: A Guide to Praying with Scripture.* Lanham, MD: Cowley, 1989.

Soelle, Dorothee. *The Silent Cry: Mysticism and Resistance.* Minneapolis: Fortress Press, 2001.

Taylor, Barbara Brown. *Holy Envy: Finding God in the Faith of Others.* New York: HarperOne, 2019.

Toner, Jules J. "The Deliberation That Started the Jesuits: A Commentario on the *Deliberatio primorum Patrum.*" *Studies in the Spirituality of Jesuits* 6, no. 4 (June 1974): 179–212.

Underhill, Evelyn. "The Parish Priest and the Life of Prayer." In *The Mount of Purification.* London: Longmans, Green, 1960.

Wilder, Amos. *Theopoetic: Theology and Religious Imagination.* Lima, OH: Academic Renewal Press, 2001.

Williams, Rowan. *The Dwelling of the Light: Praying with Icons of Christ.* Grand Rapids, MI: William B. Eerdmans, 2003.

———. *The Edge of Words: God and the Habits of Language.* London: Bloomsbury, 2014.

———. *On Christian Theology.* Malden, MA: Blackwell Publishing, 2000.

———. *The Wound of Knowledge.* London: Darton, Longman & Todd 1979. Revised edition, London: Darton, Longman & Todd, 1990.

Wilson, Jeff. *Mindful America: The Mutual Transformation of Buddhist Meditation and American Culture.* New York: Oxford University Press, 2014.

Winston, Diane et al. "Forum: What Does Mindfulness Mean for Buddhism?" *Lion's Roar* (May 5, 2015). http://www.lionsroar.com/forum -what-does-mindfulness-mean-for-buddhism/.

About the Author

Stuart Higginbotham serves as the rector of Grace Episcopal Church in Gainesville, Georgia. He received his master's in divinity from Columbia Theological Seminary and his Doctor of Ministry degree from the School of Theology at the University of the South. He also completed the clergy leadership program with the Shalem Institute for Spiritual Formation. His ongoing parish work and research focuses on the intersection of contemplative practices and congregational development, as well as interfaith studies, especially with Tibetan Buddhism. He has taught and led retreats with several organizations, including Shalem, Contemplative Outreach, the World Community for Christian Meditation, Mepkin Abbey, and the Candler School of Theology. He is the coeditor of *Contemplation and Community: A Gathering of Fresh Voices for a Living Tradition* and writes regularly at www.contemplativereformation.com.

Also by Stuart Higginbotham

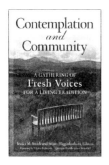

Contemplation and Community
A Gathering of Fresh Voices for a
Living Tradition

Edited by Jessica M. Smith and
Stuart Higginbotham
Foreword by Tilden Edwards
Afterword by Margaret Benefiel

All around the world, a resurgence of Christian contemplative living is creating a new framework for spirituality inside and outside of formal religion. Building on and expanding from the work of Richard Rohr, Thomas Keating, Tilden Edwards, Laurence Freeman, and other founding members of the modern contemplative movement, a new movement carries on the work of their mentors. This collection introduces the diverse voices who have emerged as new leaders of the contemplative movement. They explore such themes as silence, imagination, meditation, embodiment, community, and social action, and reflect globally on the gifts, challenges, differences, and commonalities of Christian contemplation today for communities and people of faith.

5.5 x 8.5, 288 pages   Quality Paperback   978-0824550516

"Read this book . . . to engage this deep way of knowing God . . . to bless the passing of the torch from one generation to the next . . . to see how people around the world are [engaging the wisdom of other traditions] with faith. Whatever your reason, I am pretty sure you will read it more than once."
— **Barbara Brown Taylor**, author, *Holy Envy: Finding God in the Faith of Others*

"Express[es] an exciting vision of a courageous, inclusive and prophetic contemplative Christianity witnessing . . . the change of heart and mind that humanity is called to embrace."
— **Laurence Freeman, OSB**, director, World Community for Christian Meditation